MY
JOB AND
MY
FAITH

MY
JOB AND
MY
FAITH

Twelve Christians Report on Their Work Worlds

FREDERICK K. WENTZ, EDITOR

Abingdon Press

NASHVILLE   NEW YORK

MY JOB AND MY FAITH

Copyright © 1967 by Abingdon Press

Library of Congress Catalog Card Number: 67-22169

The article on p. 131 is an abridged version of
"In All Our Doings," by Paul Wilbur. Reprinted
from *Christian Education Findings*, Vol. X, No. 6,
copyright © 1962 by The Seabury Press, Inc.

SET UP, PRINTED, AND BOUND BY THE
PARTHENON PRESS, AT NASHVILLE,
TENNESSEE, UNITED STATES OF AMERICA

*To all those laymen who have learned
to live out their Christian faith at their daily work*

FOREWORD

It is tough for a Christian to relate his faith to his daily work. Yet genuinely Christian living in the work world is one of the cutting edges of the church's mission today. For a decade I have been looking into this subject and have deplored the lack of Christian guidance and specific encouragement for laymen at their jobs. I have written a general and illustrated description of the layman's role in his secular life from the Christian perspective.[1] But living examples are the best instruction—not for copying but for suggestion and encouragement.

Many Christians are frustrated in trying to express their faith within the work situation. Others are fulfilling a Christian calling at their jobs in marvelous but unheralded ways. It is hard to find those who both live the Christian life and can describe it in a way helpful to others. The authors of the following chapters have been sought out through a variety

[1] *The Layman's Role Today* (Nashville: Abingdon Press [Apex Books], 1963).

7

of recommendations. They do not claim great success, either at their jobs or at their Christian witness. But they have described their convictions and actions candidly and interestingly. I believe their stories provide a valuable resource for other laymen who can read them and then take heart for their own Christian vocation.

All the chapters were written specifically for this volume except that of Paul Wilbor. Each author was originally confronted with the same questions, though each was encouraged to take his own approach in his own style. The four questions (with the last one considered optional to the assignment) are:

1. What is your job and what does it mean to you?
2. What are the kinds of routine decisions your job requires you to make?
3. What do you consider to be the Christian dimensions of those decisions?
4. What do you consider to be the major resources available to you as you make the decisions your job requires?

Chapter titles have been chosen by the editor, who wishes to acknowledge the help of his father, Abdel Ross Wentz, in editing several of the manuscripts, as well as the help of a number of people in suggesting laymen to be contributors to this volume.

FREDERICK K. WENTZ

CONTENTS

9

TO WALK WITH
EACH ONE

Cecelia Newbold

For many people there is a real problem of being a Christian in their work. In some occupations they cannot equate their belief and what is required of them on the job. This is not a major problem in the profession of nursing, for nursing is based on the Judeo-Christian concept of personal concern for one another. The whole ethos of the Bible is a compassion for other people. The requirements for a nurse are much the same as some of those for a Christian: to have a genuine concern for people, regardless of their racial and cultural background, education, state of mind and behavior, personality

11

and attitude, manners and morals, state of health, cleanliness of body, etc. A nurse (or a Christian) must honestly believe that every man is an individual, and it is a personal responsibility to help others to maintain their dignity and integrity through love.

In order to convey what being a nurse means to me, I must make clear that it is not a job but a way of life. You may meet women who once *were* teachers or secretaries or clerks, but if you meet a nurse, she *is* a nurse. She may be in a doctor's office, in teaching, in research, in an institutional facility, or she may be inactive, but she is still a nurse. She does not become a nurse when she fastens her starched cap on her head and dons her uniform, and she does not lose her identity when she returns to street clothes.

A nurse must have a firm grounding in all facets of human relationships, knowing how to communicate, listen, be sensitive to moods, interpret and serve needs creatively. She must have a working knowledge of biological, social, and physical sciences; but more than that, she must have a clear understanding of all the aspects of racial, social, and religious factors which have to do with well-being. A part of the preparation and education of a nurse is designed to equip her to relate to people, whether they are healthy or unhealthy, normal or abnormal, in a hospital or in a community. This "nursing equipment" is a part of her life as a woman, wife, mother, churchwoman, neighbor, community worker, and nursing Christian.

The people in one neighborhood wondered why one of the women who had always enjoyed cooking for the church, PTA, and Scouts suddenly refused either to bake or to serve for any group. She wouldn't even bake her special holiday cookies for distribution to her friends. When I visited her she initiated a conversation about this, explaining to me what she would not explain to neighbors or her minister. She had recently been diagnosed as having a disease which was unfamiliar to her. Her doctor, pressed for time, gave her a rather quick explanation, telling her so much in such a short time that she was confused. He was called out of the office and unable to answer her questions properly. She filled in her incomplete understanding with misconceptions about her condition. She felt she was "unclean" and unable to handle or cook food for anyone to eat. In listening to her I could understand her fears but, more important, could guide her thinking out of the despair she felt because I knew she misunderstood the doctor. It was a simple matter to arrange an appointment with her physician in order for him to interpret the disease, its effect on her life and habits, and to give her an opportunity to have her questions answered in an unhurried session.

As a young woman I made a choice of a career in nursing, considering what was expected of me and weighing these expectations against my abilities and potentialities. But until I was actually involved in a clinical situation I couldn't evaluate my strength of ability or purpose. As time went on, I discovered that as a nurse I was more than a therapeutic agent or a liaison between doctor and patient, but was a close confidante of personal information, a participant rather than just an observer in a patient's life, a mother image, a physical contact with the living world (to the dying), a teacher and

13

a friend. Through the years many of the lessons my patients taught me have been a resource to draw upon; their testing of my abilities has strengthened my purpose; their life-sharing relationships have been a ministry to me.

In a hospital situation it is necessary to know how to deal with conflict in many forms. Patients frequently are in conflict with themselves, their feelings, their reactions to pain, to disease, to illness. They may be irritated with the service and action of the medical staff and with other patients. Illness and hospitalization put stresses on family relationships, and at times there may be painful conflicts with those they love. Working with these realities gives a nurse insight into causes and effects of conflicts which apply also outside a hospital.

In one community a minister wondered why one of the members of his congregation was so cruelly critical in recent months. The man continually attacked the leadership of the church which he felt was far below the standards he had set as an elected lay leader a few years before. He criticized his co-workers at the office and his associates in the scouting troop he had organized, for not assuming a full load of responsibility. He felt his family was expecting too much of him in house-hold and family affairs. Many of his criticisms were inappropriate and ungrounded and were causing strain on his relationships in several arenas of his life. The minister had tried without success to reconcile this man to those he alienated. Knowing something of the man's medical background, I realized his attitudes were part of the syndrome of degeneration in a chronic disease he had. Physical deterioration and loss of ability were becoming evident to the man, and this constant source of worry and fear were reflected in his stabbing at the world with critical barbs. Without having to go into details or revealing privileged information, I could help the perplexed minister to see that this man was not being just difficult or obstructive, but that his attitude was a manifestation of a deteriorating physical condition. The minister drew on additional resources to give strength and understanding to the man and his family and to seek new directions in his ministry to them.

In the past my nursing has taken me into the arenas of the army, doctor's office, hospital, and private duty. To avoid obsolescence during the years when my children were very small, it was necessary to maintain an interested outlook and an active curiosity in nursing trends. The field of nursing is ever widening to include such specialties as coronary care with electronic monitoring equipment, aero-space medicine, research, etc., but there are still many patients that require professional bedside care by general duty or private duty nurses.

Nursing is an art as well as a science. It is not a field of self-sacrifice, but rather an area of ministry to others that gives the greatest personal satisfaction. People need people, not only to meet their own needs but to be needed by others. The relationship of patient and nurse is unlike any other, and a part of its uniqueness is the intimacy with which one relates to a person. It is in this dimension—sharing another's concerns by serving the whole person—that bedside nursing brings immeasurable rewards.

Because of additional responsibilities I have assumed in

my denomination and community, my institutional nursing has been somewhat limited in recent months. I call my current nursing "bouquet nursing" and "bottom of the barrel nursing."

Bouquet nursing is the term I use for caring for a friend or acquaintance for an eight-hour shift (or several) following surgery or in a period of crisis. I feel that professional bedside nursing is the gift I can best give, and this is my "bouquet of flowers." In order to do this, I always consult with the friend (or family) and check with the doctor and floor supervisor. I indicate my nonprofit nursing status and have a clear understanding with the staff in regard to duties to assume or share with the nursing team assigned to the patient.

Bottom of the barrel nursing is the result of an arrangement with a nearby hospital to the effect that when they have exhausted the nursing registry list and their reserve list, they call me. When they call, I know they are "scraping the bottom of the barrel" and that it is a critical situation. They respect my wishes to be called only as a last resort, and I make every effort to arrange my affairs to respond to their call.

As I review many of my past bottom of the barrel cases, I find that almost all were critical, emergency or terminal. Because each case begins in crisis, I have a particularly close relationship with my patients and their families. There is a communication between nurse and critical patient unlike that in any other relationship. Doctors may see their patients on hospital rounds for a few minutes in the morning and evening; family may visit for many hours, but this is an emotional stress on both patient and family. The nurse spends eight hours in a special dimension of "caring." I have learned to adapt myself readily wherever I am and whatever I'm doing. My patient is an essential part of my life for the time I'm on his case.

Nursing duties are quite carefully delineated as to orientation to the history of the case, prescribed therapy, medication, laboratory and nursing procedures, observation, evaluation and reporting technics, etc., but each patient is a real personality, not just a human organism. At the beginning of each case, it is necessary to prepare the care for the patient. In some hospitals there is a chapel, and it is a simple matter to step in for a prayer for the patient, the family, the doctor, and for myself as I minister to my patient. If there is no chapel, my prayer may be a quick and simple one as I ride in the elevator or walk down the hall toward his room.

Other preparation consists of careful reading of his chart. A picture of the patient begins to form as I read his name, age, occupation, place of birth, his marital status. A part of the picture is his medical history; the childhood diseases and accidents he has suffered, the surgery performed upon him in the past. Then the current condition: the onset and history, the lab reports, consultation studies. Reading the medication and treatment orders adds to the composite picture of the patient. The previous nurse has noted information about his vital signs (his blood pressure, pulse, and respirations), indicated her observations of his response to treatment and her evaluation of his condition. When I enter his room he is "Mr. Smith," no longer an unknown person, for I know about him and his family and his history. In crisis situations Mr. Smith is the *real* Mr. Smith, for the defenses of his lifetime are weakened and, as a privileged companion, I see the best or worst of Mr. Smith, for he is quite defenseless.

Many patients (and their families) enter the hospital feeling that pain is punishment or penalty, and that death is the ultimate punishment. Some people never accept the fact that pain is universal and that everyone feels pain, though reactions differ. Since pain cannot be separated from emotions, it is not enough to give medications. Pain must be "managed" by certain nursing technics and arts, and by giving emotional support and strength. Patients need help to understand their pain and their reaction of anxiety and hostility to it.

One of the major concerns of the patient and his family is the imminence of death. It is apparent to me that most people, no matter what their religious background, are inadequately prepared for the ultimate fact of death for themselves and their families. The church, both clergy and laity, needs a better understanding and interpretation of the Christian hope. Some preparation is essential if the message of the gospel is to have any significance at times of crisis.

Although as a nurse I am not required to provide a spiritual ministry to patients, to ignore a patient's religious background or his relationship to God would do a disservice to the whole man. I need an awareness of the meaning of religion to support the patient in his use of his religious beliefs. I must accept differences in religious beliefs and realize the influence of my religious beliefs in dealing with my patients.

Extension of life by extraordinary means in the moribund patient is an area of continuing concern, as its frequency increases due to improved methods of prolonging life. The nurse's role is not in the decision of extension of life, but in calling upon available resources to counsel the family, that they may make the decisions.

Some time ago I had a patient who was nearing the end of his life. He was over ninety years of age, in terminal condition, suffering from severe internal hemorrhages which did not respond to therapy. He was semiconscious; occasionally he would rouse during treatment or movement or in response to a voice. During one of his conscious moments he expressed concern for his grieving family. He said he had lived a long and wonderful life, was happy, was tired, and was ready to die. To the doctor and intern and to me he expressed his gratitude for care and concern. He was prepared to die.

But the consultants on the medical team felt that life must be extended if at all possible. So further treatment was initiated in addition to measures being used to give comfort and to relieve pain.

The family struggled with their feelings, on the one hand, that he should be given all the medical attention necessary and available at any cost, knowing that his condition was irreversible, and, on the other, to let him die with some of the dignity of a man who is prepared and ready to meet death. When I informed the doctor of their distress, he arranged to meet with them and the minister in a quiet private room away from the patient. The doctor, the family, and the minister together were able to arrive at a decision in Christian faith, to continue to ease but not to prolong the pain and discomfort of a dying man. The old gentleman died after a time. He was given medication to ease his pain, oxygen to aid his breathing, but the transfusions, intravenous fluids, and painful treatments and other medications were discontinued.

After such decisions are made, supportive measures are a part of the ministry to the family. This kind of nursing includes not just the body, mind, and spirit of the patient but the family as well.

I have always felt that a comatose patient is much more aware of what is said and done in his presence than has been believed in the past. I talk to my unconscious patient. I greet him when I come into the room, tell him my name, and express aloud the hope that I can serve to make him more comfortable and to help him regain his health. When I turn a patient for nursing procedures, treatment, or medication, I tell him that I'm going to move him, that there may be some discomfort, but that this procedure will help to make him more comfortable or aid in his recovery. During the day I tell him of the beauty of the day, the view from the window, the loveliness of the flowers in his room. I request all visitors to speak only the words they would want the patient to hear, for I believe he can hear.

Not long ago I had a patient who had attempted suicide by an overdose of drugs. She was in a deep coma and had not responded to any stimuli or therapy, and her prognosis was guarded. When I came on the case, the resident physician indicated that she had been comatose for a long period of time and that not much hope was held for her recovery.

As I cared for her that day, I talked to her from time to time in a quiet voice about one of the Greek Islands in the Aegean Sea which is a favorite place of mine. I suggested that if she were to walk with me up that heather covered hill, we could see the entire island. So I described the feel of the rough textured heather on our legs as we walked through it. I described the color of the heather plants and the pungent fragrance. I tried to convey the feeling of the warmth of the sun and the clear sweet air so characteristic of Greece. I told her of the inhabitants of the island, the little donkeys and peacocks, and how their voices were intermingled with the sea sounds and buzzing of insects. And then we "walked" down the other side of the hill, under the olive trees and onto the white sand, and stood looking out at the incredibly blue sea.

For the first time since her admittance she began to move. Her legs moved in a rhythmic way. Her knee would bend and then the leg extend, and then the other, and they moved alternately. I realized she was "walking."

In time she recovered and went home. I saw her from a distance once and wondered if she had any memories of hearing about the little Greek island of Moni.

I feel that the human touch, one person to another, is important in expressing concern and caring. In moments of stress, pain, anxiety, to hold a patient's hand gives a feeling of strength to him. And through a patient's hand I have "felt" some of the pain and sorrow and strength of another person. It is a way of showing love, and love is the most healing experience.

To say there are no problems in nursing would be unrealistic, for dealing with people is conflict-provoking. But the conflicts are with people, not with the profession.

Occasionally a hospital or doctor or head nurse will expect a nurse to perform medical or paramedical procedures which are not within the scope of nursing. Usually this involves a procedure which has been accepted as a matter of course for many years. But acceptance by the hospital does not make it legal, and proper channels are available for resolution of such problems. When I take a case in an unfamiliar hospital, I request an orientation which includes a clear definition about certain "gray areas" of accepted practice. Most hospitals now have established rules based on the state nursing laws.

The means for reporting nonprofessional behavior or variance from professional standards by medical or nursing personnel are provided in most hospitals. A nurse need not participate in any unethical procedure and in no instance can be compelled to do anything contrary to her conscience. Nursing ethics do not demand that a nurse protect either a patient or hospital worker if a criminal act is involved. If there is any suspicion of a crime like criminal abortion, narcotic law violation, criminal abuse of children, or gun shot wounds, the case is reportable. Where the law is concerned the duty is quite clear. A nurse is responsible for her own act. In fact she can refuse to perform a procedure because she is not qualified to do it, or because the order came from a person exceeding his authority. It is always right for a nurse to act according to her conscience, but she needs an understanding of legal and ethical codes as well. Many conflicts and dilemmas can be avoided by clear definition of duties at the time of employment, by tact and by common sense, but nursing associations have legal counsel available in case of legal jeopardy. The nurse is under obligation to conduct herself according to high professional standards, which may require more of her than the standards society sets for its members.

A few years ago, while visiting in Turkey, I entered the tower room of an old military fort in Uskadar. This had been the quarters of Florence Nightingale which she used during the Crimean War when she and thirty-seven nurses cared for British soldiers in this installation. Her room is unlocked only a few times during the year for an occasional visitor. The musty room held only a desk and some pictures of the "Angel of the Crimea," a bouquet of dead flowers (sent several months before on the anniversary of her birthday), and a few letters and diaries she had written. As I leafed through the fragile pages, one phrase in her handwriting caught my eye: "To be a good nurse one must first be a good woman." To be a nursing Christian, or a Christian nurse, to meet a person's physiological and psychological needs, whether he is patient, neighbor, friend, or stranger, to care for his life and inevitable death is a lifetime challenge.

It requires a fine skill which can never be perfected. In a sense, every "nursing Christian" must meet the same challenge: to meet man's needs, to minister to him with the abilities and skills that are a part of the equipment of each person.

THAT THE WORLD MAY BE
FASHIONED ANEW *Norman E. Madson*

"Christianity is more than a Sunday affair" is a comment
I have heard many times since early childhood. It is usually
intended to mean that a man's faith should affect his activities
every day of the week and in all parts of his life. To some
this statement means that, if you don't use profanity on
Sunday, you shouldn't on Tuesday. To others it means that
about the middle of each week you should attend Bible
study at the church. To some it means that the kindness
toward others that you hear about on Sunday should be

demonstrated during the week by special acts of kindness to those about you.

Of course it means all these things, but it ought to mean much more. It ought also to include an understanding of the relationship of faith to the routine matters of life. Seldom do we hear that the Christian faith has anything to do with the way a painter paints, a teacher teaches, or a salesman sells. Much is said about taking advantage of a particular situation for evangelism, but little is said about what our attitude ought to be toward our work. Yet if we believe that God is God of all life we believe that this is his world and it is here we are meant to serve him, including the manner in which we perform our daily tasks. In order to explore the relationship of faith and life in my particular situation, I will attempt to answer these questions: What is my job? What routine decisions am I required to make? What are the Christian dimensions of these decisions?

My Job

I am an architect in partnership with two others in a medium-size firm in the Upper Midwest. Our staff consists of twenty-four architects and draftsmen who together with the secretaries and office help make a total staff of thirty. Ours is a general practice in that our work includes the design of a variety of types and sizes of buildings. Churches and church related buildings have occupied a large portion of our time and efforts, but our work also includes college buildings such as dormitories, libraries, student centers, music halls, administration buildings, and athletic centers. Nursing homes, residences, apartment buildings, and commercial and industrial buildings have also been planned. Most of the buildings we plan are constructed in the Midwest where we hold architectural licenses in twelve states; however, buildings have also been planned recently for clients in Pennsylvania, Alaska, and Norway. Each of the partners is a member of the American Institute of Architects as are the other registered men on our staff, most of whom are college graduates with architectural degrees. We employ professional consultants outside our office for structural, mechanical, and electrical engineering, as well as other specialists.

Perhaps a brief outline of the basic steps involved with a typical project in our office would help to describe my work. In most instances new work is secured by responding to inquiries from an individual or a group who plan to erect a new building. During the first meeting we discuss the proposed project and explain fully our services and fees. When selected for a project, the architect and the owner enter into a written agreement which explains clearly the obligations of each party. The first step taken by the architect is to become completely familiar with the needs of the client and the site on which the building is to be erected. In most instances a written report or "program" is prepared, discussed, and revised before any sketches are started. If a factory is being planned, the architect must understand the processes and spaces required as the material moves from stock to finished product. The designer of a school must know not only the number of students per class and the

27

total number to be accommodated, but also how the teaching will be done, and he must have an understanding of the relationship of spaces. A good program for any building will treat in considerable detail the ideas, attitudes, and philosophies of those who will use it.

The first set of drawings is called "schematic drawings" in which the architect translates the needs as described in the "program" into a plan which also takes into account the topography of the site and the soil conditions. Requirements of the state and local building codes are also considered early in the planning stages. The schematic drawings show little detail but deal primarily with the basic requirements.

When the architect and owner arrive at a basic scheme which seems to provide the right solution, the drawings are prepared in more detail, and more attention is given to the specific materials to be used. This stage of planning is called "design development." Now the architect's drawings are correlated with those of the engineers and an outline specification of materials is prepared as well as an estimate of the costs. At the completion of the design development phase, the drawings and specifications describe the building in sufficient detail so that all parties have a clear understanding of what is proposed.

When the design development drawings are approved, the "working drawings and specifications" are prepared. These are the drawings from which the builders compute the construction costs in order to place a bid on the work and the ones used for the actual construction. A set of working drawings for a typical building would include a site plan, floor plans, exterior and interior elevations, sections through the building, and large-scale and accurately detailed drawings of stairways, door frames, special millwork items and numerous other details. In addition to the architectural drawings a complete set of working drawings would include drawings which show the structural, mechanical, and electrical requirements. Many pages of written specifications which describe in detail the quality of workmanship and materials required accompany the working drawings.

When the working drawings and specifications are completed, the architect assists the owner in the selection of the contractors. In some instances the contractors are selected without competitive bidding; in other instances bids are received from a selected list of contractors; and usually on public projects the bidding is open to all who are interested and qualified. During the construction period the architect makes periodic trips to the site to see that the drawings and specifications are properly interpreted and carried out by the contractor. Shop drawings prepared by steel companies, millwork shops, and other suppliers are checked by the architect for compliance with the architectural drawings and specifications before the items are fabricated and delivered to the job site. The contractor's monthly requests for payment are checked and approved before payments are made by the owner, as are proposals for changes.

This outline is extremely brief, but it will help to show that a typical building project requires a close working relationship between the architect and numerous others: the client, which in some instances includes several committees and subcommittees, professional consultants for the engineering requirements, contractors, subcontractors, material suppliers, manufacturer's representatives and, of course, numerous members of his own staff. The successful completion of a project requires not only architectural abilities but also the ability to coordinate the interests and concerns of all those involved, through much correspondence and numerous conferences as well as through the drawings.

Routine Decisions

In order to discuss the typical decisions involved, I will describe a few loosely related issues which we face regularly.

Small Projects. What should our attitude as an office be toward accepting small difficult projects? It is true in our work, as it is in most other businesses and professions, that it is extremely difficult to avoid losing money on small projects, since the number of meetings, the amount of travel, and the time required for processing the project are much greater in proportion to the cost of the work and consequently to the fee collected. While the percentage fees are greater for small, difficult work, they are usually not enough greater to cover the additional expenses. Budget allowances are usually tighter on small projects and require a reduction in the quality of the building in order to provide as much area as possible. Should we simply make a clear business decision and avoid such work, or do we have some responsibility to provide service where needed? The question is not whether we should design a building to be built too cheaply

—clearly a disservice to the client—but rather, should we, though recognizing the problem in advance, spend the time and take the loss required to see that a good though small building is built?

Design Time. How much time should be spent on the early design stages? It is usually much easier and therefore less costly to design a building which satisfies the client than it is to satisfy ourselves. Many people have preconceived ideas of what the building should be in both plan and exterior appearance, and the time required to draw it that way is not great; however, since such preconceived ideas usually neither take into account adequately all requirements of the program nor take advantage of the site, a competent architect who struggles seriously with the problem can ordinarily arrive at a better solution. The receptiveness of clients to new schemes varies considerably; it is not uncommon to spend a great deal of time and money persuading the client to accept a better solution than the one he had in mind. Some will say that it is the owner's money and he should be able to get what he wants. But a doctor would not remove an appendix if he knew that the trouble was with the gall bladder, even if ordered to do so by his patient. Neither should an architect permit his client to build the wrong building. While we must guard constantly to make certain that our decisions are based on sound judgment resulting from years of study and experience and not merely on our own set of prejudices, we are often required to spend hundreds of hours beyond the point where the client is satisfied in order to arrive at the right design.

New Materials. There has been a phenomenal advancement through the years in the development of new materials for building construction. While most of them have been developed by manufacturers, their success has been dependent upon the architects' willingness to try them in new construction. The result is that society has benefited greatly from this process. However, difficulties with the use of new materials is one of the most common causes for law suits against architects. What should our attitude be toward the use of new construction materials? As architects we have some responsibility for their development if there is to be progress in this area. No competent architect will take unnecessary risks, but the only way to avoid nearly all risk is to avoid new materials until others have tested them over a period of years, and consequently abandon all responsibility for their development. The question is, "How safe do you play it, especially when the new product, if it performs as intended, would serve your client better at less cost?"

Completeness of Drawings. The architect is concerned that his client receive full value for the money spent. One of the best ways to insure this is to prepare the detailed plans and specifications so thoroughly that no questions are left unanswered. This work well done is costly to the architect, but it enables the contractors to prepare more accurate bids and helps to eliminate costly extras during construction. If the plans and specifications are not complete and clear, the contractor who prepares a bid must add an amount to his bid to cover the uncertainties. It is possible, however, to furnish plans that are less complete than they ought to be,

32

but protect yourself with a "blanket clause" in the specifications which requires the contractor to furnish the material and labor necessary to complete the work whether completely detailed or not. It is ironical that an architect's relationship with his client may be better when he protects himself with a blanket clause, even if it is more costly to the client.

Let me cite an example: An architect prepares a carefully detailed set of drawings with a clear, unambiguous set of specifications. A contractor submits a bid of $100,000 for the work, and the contract is awarded. In spite of his efforts to include everything needed on the plans and specifications, an item was overlooked and it becomes necessary to allow the contractor an extra $2,000 during the construction period. The owner agrees reluctantly to pay it but feels that the architect has given something less than the best service. An architect with less concern for the owner's welfare and more concern for his own prepares a set of drawings for a similar building in considerably less detail and therefore at less cost to his own office, but he includes a "blanket clause" in the specifications to cover those items not clearly shown on the drawings. When the contractor prepares his bid he realizes that there are items which are not clearly described and whose actual cost therefore is not known. In order to cover the cost of the known and unknown items, he adds a protective sum and submits a bid of $110,000. When the unseen items arise during the construction period, no extra is allowed because the clause in the specifications makes it the contractor's responsibility to include enough in his bid to cover them. While the owner paid $10,000 for a $2,000 item, he believes that his architect served him well because no extras were required. There is an obvious temptation to operate in a way which protects oneself at others' expense. Architects must work at each project within the framework of these tensions. How much time can we afford to spend to make the drawings perfectly clear? How can we protect the owner from costly extras during construction without having a larger amount included in the original bids?

Bid-Shopping. Some difficult decisions are often involved during the bidding period of construction projects. Before a general contractor can submit a bid on a project, he must first receive numerous subbids for material and some of the labor items. Subbids would be received for structural steel, windows, roofing and sheet metal, glass and glazing, floor covering, painting, masonry work, and many other items. In order for the owner to receive the lowest bids possible, it is necessary that the contractors first receive the best possible subbids. Unfortunately, when the successful contractor becomes known, there is sometimes a period of vicious price slashing among the subbidders. Someone who submitted a subbid of $12,000 will reduce it to $11,600 which puts him $100 below the previous low bidder. After the subbidders discover that a general contractor allows bid-shopping after the contract is awarded, they usually decide not to submit their price on the next project until they know who the successful contractor is, or, if they do, they allow enough in their bid to enable them to negotiate for a lower price later on. In either case it means that the general contractor does not have the best price at the time of the bidding, and therefore the cost to the owner is greater. Many reliable contractors have taken steps to correct this situation by signing a bidding code in which they agree not to accept or change the amounts of subbids after the letting. This means that if a subbidder wants the job he must submit his best price the first time, and he must submit it before the general contractor submits his bid to the owner. Architects support and encourage this procedure since it clarifies the bidding process and assures the owner of the best price. Suppose that the low bid submitted on a project is $1,500,000 and the contracts are awarded. Soon one of the subcontractors, who bid on the finish hardware but was not the low subbidder, lowers his bid enough to cut out the previous low bidder by $1,500. The general contractor suggests to the architect that he will give the owner a credit of $1,000 if the substitution in the make of hardware is allowed. The architect knows that the hardware is equal to that specified, but he also knows that the savings resulted from unscrupulous bid-cutting. He is faced with the decision: should he allow the change or not? If he does, it will mean a savings of $1,000 to his client without any reduction in quality of the building, but it will contribute to a practice which leads to higher costs for others who plan to build. Does his attitude change if the savings is $10,000?

Assignment of Work. Part of my responsibility as administrative partner is the assignment of work to the staff. We

35

feel that we have a responsibility to assist in the training of future architects, and our staff usually includes some recent college graduates. Unless a man has had considerable office experience during his college days, his first two years are primarily a training period during which time his production is worth less than the pay he receives. Some of these new employees are quite obviously planning to spend only a few years with us and then move on, while others plan to stay on indefinitely if we want them. Should I be affected by my understanding of their future plans when assigning work? Is the man who plans to stay only a short while entitled to the same variety of broadening assignments as the one who will stay to contribute to the firm? Where is the proper balance between our desire to assist in a man's training and our need to operate efficiently? We operate more efficiently with inexperienced personnel when we have them perform the same tasks many times, rather than when we assign them a variety of tasks which would broaden their experience. Some of these same considerations for a man's total experience through a variety of types and sizes of projects apply also when assigning work to the permanent staff. The assigning of work always requires a consideration of what is best for the individual as well as what is economically possible for the firm.

The Character of the Architecture. If the architect is immersed in complexities in his relation to all his dealings with the people on his staff and outside it, he is also caught in a web of complexities in relation to the building itself. The following paragraphs printed in our office brochure set forth the concept of design which has guided our work.

Architecture is a shelter for human activities, and as such convenience, durability and economy are ideals. On this agreement is general. Architecture is also an esthetic problem. On this problem opinion is various.

We see architectural esthetics as concerned not simply with the effort to make a sensually pleasant and delightful environment. Architecture is a subtle, persuasive and expressive language of ideas and values, an art of meaning and communication. It can provide an environment which teaches, influences, and carries on a dialogue with people; it can meet people in intellectual, ethical and ideological arenas, through sensibilities which are rational and otherwise.

Thus a church building is not simply a pleasant place which shelters worshippers; it can be an expressive medium which emphasizes, echoes and reiterates in visual form the ideas and values about which a congregation gathers. A school building is not simply a useful and pleasant shelter in which teaching is done; the building itself can be a teacher, articulating the concepts which an educational system hopes to establish in scholars.

An institutional building is not simply a nice place where concerned people can care for and minister to others; the building itself can be expressive and demonstrative of kindness and concern.

The history of architecture indicates that the great work of the past is not simply useful and pleasant, but meaningful as well, and that great builders were men of great faith, understanding and conscience, as well as skill and sensitivity. If this is true significant architecture now will also come from sources which are profoundly conscious of the ideals and values of human life and destiny.

If a building is, as we believe, an image of ideas, values, hopes, attitudes, how does the Christian architect witness through it to the faith which sustains him? We assert that as Christians we deplore deceits, affectations, artificialities, and insincerities and are committed to truth. The American environment is in any number of ways an artificial one or partly so, and our clients are generally content with it, having become half-blind to most of the common artifices. This puts the architect in a constant tension. A very unsophisticated example may be drawn from the use of plastics in buildings. We are all familiar with the wood-grained plastic sheathing which is used in furniture and as a finish for other surfaces. It is useful, attractive, inexpensive, durable, and a very skillful imitation of the real thing. It shocks most clients to learn that we consider its use, and a host of other imitative materials and techniques of construction, deceitful and unworthy of honest people. It shocks them even more if we propose to use, as we sometimes must, materials which are either more expensive or less durable, or some which most people consider less attractive. At innumerable points, most of them much more subtle than this example, the conscientious architect must spend himself persuading his client that he cannot tolerate the untruthful and the unreal, and that a concern for integrity, in this sense, is a good investment.

Suppose an architect is designing the interior of a clothing store. Currently our commercial enterprises are caught up with a variety of display gimmicks. Stores are done in colonial motifs, ranch house motifs, and many other clever, cheap, and easy artifices. One rarely enters a store which is simply a good store. And retailers know that this kind of merchandising device works, no matter how devious it is. Can an architect who is a Christian undertake to participate in ventures of this sort when he knows that they are contributing to the general artificiality of our environment and our lives?

The architect is an artist. He knows that art is probably the only human enterprise which can say something directly about the existence of that category of religious experience we call the holy. But to make a building into a good work of art takes time and effort, not to speak of imagination, sensitivity, and understanding. The architect's client, more often than not, wants a building for the convenient and comfortable shelter it provides, not because he wants to be reminded of any mysterious reality, particularly when, until a project is complete, there is no assurance whether it will be a consequential work of art or not. The pressure to sacrifice the artistic values of design to those which can be measured in cost is nearly constant. When people talk about an artist's suffering they really refer to the tortures of decision and sometimes remorse that often accompany this problem. The Christian architect (and the non-Christian as well) knows that his faithfulness in this concern is the most valuable gift he can make to the world.

There are other related problems. How can he witness,

through the expressive character of his architectural project, to his faith in an orderly universe, to an order which is often so clouded as to seem absurd? How can a building be an echo of the gospel with its creative liberating character? What is the nature of form which reflects the grace and relentless kindness of God's love? What kind of spaces and shapes and colors and textures and visual rhythms say something about the Christian's faith that the Holy Spirit is active, that the work of God is continuing? What sort of architecture is it which will tell people that we believe that this world is the scene of our redemption, and will, indeed, contribute to that redemption? It is clear to a thoughtful and critical student of architectural history that most of the architectural images in history are not very helpful; most of them are static, or otherworldly, or authoritarian, or otherwise remiss. Even those forms which the church has used are generally more expressive of a natural religion than of Christianity. But the Christian's obligation is to order his work in such a way that, in the words of one of the documents of Vatican II, "the world may be fashioned anew according to God's design and reach its fulfillment."

To enter his work with this kind of concern is the most profound problem the architect faces as a Christian. It is an immensely difficult problem which one must approach with the certainty that he will fail. And yet, if one has defined the problem, the failure is not likely to be so great as it would be otherwise. There may even be minor successes along the way.

The projects on which the architect works will usually

be standing long after the problems of dealing with client, staff, and builders have passed out of memory. Therefore the witness the project *itself* makes is ultimately the means by which an architect does or does not bring his faith to fruit in his work. But along the way all the other factors inject their complexities into the achievement, and its success is dependent on hidden and indirect factors which can scarcely be numbered.

Christian Dimensions

What then are the Christian dimensions of these decisions? The world is not only the arena in which God works, but it is also the arena in which he calls men to work with him. The Christian believes that through men of faith the power of God's love can break into the sphere of the ordinary things of life. Through faith the Christian's occupation and social responsibilities become a vocation, that is, an opportunity for service to his neighbors. God does not need our service but our neighbors do, and we serve God by serving our fellowmen. Scripture makes a clear distinction between law and gospel. One lives a Christian life if he obeys the law of God in Christian faith, but the law which gives shape and direction to our lives is not a specific law which prescribes an ideal for Christians that is unknown to non-Christians. Our good works must simply be those deeds which fulfill our neighbors' needs; and our neighbors' needs are human needs. These deeds are not specifically or uniquely Christian, since human needs have always existed and will always

41

exist, whether Christians are present or not, and the actions that satisfy the real needs of men are not changed in character or aim because they are done by a Christian. The Christian is not commanded to do good works other than those that every man ought to do for his neighbor—to satisfy the human needs of his neighbor. Questions that have to do with daily bread and freedom, with education and sanitation, with honesty and kindness and fairplay in business, government, school, and home are human problems—not Christian problems. But just because they are human problems they are of endless and costly concern for Christian men. As we work out our obligation in society and in our routine daily tasks, there is no peculiar form of Christian duty but only a Christian urgency to do our human duty well. Unfortunately, many Christians consider the world evil, and that applies to those activities not directly related to prayer, Bible study, and worship. They believe withdrawal from a naughty world to be the best policy. Such an attitude avoids the responsibilities which rightly belong to the Christian, and leaves the world to its own self-destruction. For those who feel this way, all of life is divided into two parts—the spiritual and the worldly. One is spiritual when speaking to another of Christ, reading the Bible, or engaging in worship. One is worldly when studying, attending a political rally, negotiating with a contractor, or doing other routine daily tasks. This idea may be religious but it is not biblical. Persons in Scripture are spiritual when they take seriously their work as shepherd, king, soldier, and father. Their spirituality is measured by their faithfulness to God in the routine affairs of life. The Bible makes no distinction between World and Spirit but only between loyalties—loyalty to God or mammon. Cups of water for the thirsty, clothes for the naked, and food for the hungry could hardly be more of the world; yet Jesus designated these as spiritual services, "Inasmuch as you have done it unto the least of these, you have done it unto me." Unless the definition of spiritual service has changed since the Son of Man walked on this earth, it can be a spiritual service to plow a field, sweep a floor, teach a class, study a lesson, or design a building. As the Christian seeks to be a witness in the world, he will not know in advance what concrete forms his service will take. Although he walks in love and has permanent relationships that define his duties, he must live without a code. He has a sense of direction and a goal in mind, but he does not receive detailed instructions. Like a football player who runs the length of the field, he knows the goal but he does not know in advance exactly what he will encounter along the way or what action will be necessary. Or, as Paul told the Philippians, "With hands outstretched to whatever lies ahead I go straight for the goal—my reward the honor of being called by God in Christ." The Christian must use his individual opportunities and his individual talents in freedom to witness effectively to the love of God in a fallen world. He will nearly always be involved in situations where simple judgments of black and white are not adequate. Rather, he will be in a broad "gray" area of moral decision where he must choose the lesser evil. He will have to act in faith and for love without any guarantee that he is doing the right thing. But since he is covered by the forgiveness of God he is free to assume responsibility, even though social action and the routine decisions of his daily work will always involve aspects of evil. When we understand that we serve God when we serve our fellowmen, then all that we do has a Christian dimension—even the routine decisions of an ordinary day.

A BOY
PRAYED FOR A GOOD JOB *Louis R. Mobley*

What Is My Job and What Does It Mean to Me?

This is a particularly interesting question to try to answer. I guess most men in our culture consider their job to be quite important in their lives. I do too.

Before I was twelve years old, I would customarily add to my bedtime prayers the request that someday I might have a good job. Having grown up in a family that considered itself Christian, it seemed natural to pray for the things that were important to my life. Of all the things I hoped for as a child, a good job was top priority.

To get my college education, I had to work my way through school. But these jobs did not seem to be "the job." That was still in the future. I became a cooperative student in order to earn my college expenses. Depression years and my one objective—to get a degree—combined to make of these jobs temporary arrangements to accomplish a specific economic objective.

At graduation I was interviewed by IBM and given a job as customer engineer in Atlanta. It never occurred to me that anyone made his own job; I took it for granted that I must become an employee of some company. I felt I was not ready, but this company had a training program which seemed particularly attractive.

Was this the job that I considered to be so important in earlier years? I didn't give it much thought. After all, the managers who interviewed me made me feel they wanted me. They gave me a test, which meant to me that they were choosy. I rose to the challenge and made it. I was hired!

I shall never forget that first year: being paid a salary to go to school, and travel expenses besides! Furthermore, everyone I worked with was proud of the company; I was too.

The work was fascinating; fixing IBM machines was a challenge and immensely satisfying. But was this the job for which I worked so hard to get a college degree? Within two years I wanted "administrative" work.

World War II interrupted my wishes for five years. But during those five years I had an opportunity to teach in the Army Ordnance School. I enjoyed teaching and was good at it. After the war, I requested and obtained a teaching job at IBM's school.

Each succeeding job lasted from two to five years. Each succeeding job held great satisfaction but also opened up possibilities which beckoned my interests into a new activity. In this way, my "job" in IBM changed from teaching to engineering recruitment, to education administration, to business research, to sales promotion, to executive development, to organization planning, to education manager. I have traced this history of jobs to demonstrate, at least in my case, a number of facts: My college education trained me to perform on none of those jobs, but it probably educated me to be adaptable and quickly learn how to do any of them. Over the years my "job" has not been definable along skill or professional lines except for short periods of time; rather, it has been to help IBM grow in many ways that I was able to contribute. In other words, my career job has been IBM, not engineering, or teaching, or sales. I believe I have learned much more since graduating from college than ever I learned in formal schooling. The explanation, I believe, is that in formal schooling others were deciding what was good for me; since then, the responsibility I had for certain achievements provided a motivation to learn that I never felt in formal schooling. My degree, nevertheless, served as my "entrance ticket" to being considered for "professional" types of work.

Against this background of experience, I look upon my present responsibility as Manager of Education and Development for the Federal Systems Division of IBM as my present opportunity to contribute to the growth of IBM and to my own growth.

What does this "job" mean to me now? I selected the Federal Systems Division after ten years of work at the corporate level, including five years directing IBM's executive development program. I had become intimately acquainted with the company's executives. I decided I did not wish to pay the price of climbing the higher rungs of the executive ladder: time away from my family, night work, pressure, travel, and other demands would prevent my doing many things I wanted to do which required my time and not my money.

The Federal Systems Division is engaged in solving complex, large-scale information handling problems for the federal government. It has about 10,000 employees, most of whom are professional people of great skill and talent. The management of a variety of educational programs conducted for these employees is my present assignment.

There are four centers which conduct the operations of the division at various places throughout the country. Each center has a manager of education who reports organizationally to his center general manager but reports to me in a staff relationship. Each center manager of education has a staff of educational specialists who arrange or teach a great variety of educational programs from new employee orientation to three-year resident graduate study programs and executive development programs. Most courses are offered as an opportunity for employees to upgrade and update their professional competence.

My job is to manage these educational programs of the division at the policy level. My position guide, created jointly by me and my manager, the divisional personnel director, reads as follows:

The Federal Systems Division Manager of Education and Development is responsible to the Director of Personnel for planning and evaluating all educational and training programs of the division. He is responsible for formulating divisional policies with respect to customer education, employee orientation, job training, and volunteer education programs, graduate work study programs, tuition refund programs, resident graduate study programs, and management and executive development. Responsible for Security and Safety in the division.

What this job means to me now is an opportunity to help 10,000 employees grow as individuals; this in turn helps the division to grow, and, in doing this, I grow. The specific experiences which lead to such growth may now be described in some detail.

What Are the Kinds of Routine Decisions My Job Requires Me to Make?

My present job as manager of education for 10,000 employees requires that many decisions be made every day. I find it as difficult to describe them as I would to describe the decisions I make in my daily living away from the job.

I can recall some of the decisions I have made in the last several weeks or months and hope they are fairly typical.

The more significant decisions have been those that were not made quickly or hurriedly. It took several weeks or months to obtain relevant data, check with various parties or people who would be affected by the decision, and negotiate with certain people who were opposed. I always try to be reasonably sure that the persons affected by the decision will not be surprised and will support the decision.

The case of an assistant may illustrate one of the more significant decisions I have made in recent months.

The division president and the personnel director have for some months been considering ways to strengthen the management team. Because of the nature of the division's business, a large proportion of its employees are professional people, and most of these are engineers, mathematicians, and systems designers. It is very difficult for these specialists to become managers; yet they want to be managers in order to progress.

I had agreed with the president and personnel director that I should assume a major responsibility for management effectiveness.

At about the same time, a problem had arisen with the safety director who also was part of the personnel office. Everyone in the personnel office felt that the safety director was a poor performer. I agreed to add him to my staff. He and I had decided that nine-tenths of his responsibility was to be safety, and one-tenth of his responsibility was to assist me on educational matters; his position guide reflected this division of responsibility.

But there was no way to measure his performance as safety director. He was needed in education. I made the decision: make half his job education assistant and the other half safety.

Would he accept it? If so, he would be giving up half his career as a safety expert and assume responsibility in education. I told him there was no further progress in safety in this division for him. Could the safety responsibility be carried during half his time? He made the decision to change. We rewrote his position guide, and together we wrote down some clear achievement goals in each area—safety and education.

With this educational assistance, I could turn my personal attention to management effectiveness.

The results: He accomplished his initial achievement goals and we then created more challenging goals. He worked much harder. His attitude improved. Everyone in the department agreed he was a good performer. And I could do a better job on management effectiveness.

In this case, the decision to change a man's job was preceded by several months of worrying and was followed by performance improvement on both his and my part.

The following cases illustrate routine decisions:

• Negotiated a contract with a local university to conduct a certain course for employees.

• Recommended to the president the names of executives who should participate in a variety of executive development programs.

• Conducted a management effectiveness conference for educational managers of the several plants and facilities.

• Established criteria for matching executives in the management inventory to education programs being offered.

• Briefed the executive council on the need and concepts behind appraisal by objectives.

• Visited a facility to make an educational and management audit.

51

• Decided to purchase a closed circuit educational T.V. system for one center.

• Assumed the responsibilities of my boss while he was on vacation. This led to a variety of decisions outside my regular responsibilities.

Still more routine in nature are decisions illustrated by the following situations:

• Decision to turn down a request for speaking engagement in another part of the country.

• Decision to explore the significance of a certain want advertisement placed for a headquarters executive.

• Decision to delegate the planning for a certain educational course to my assistant.

• Decision on the person to serve as resident administrator for a certain executive development course (this decision had to be changed twice because of conflicts with personal plans of the first two men selected).

What Do I Consider to Be the Christian Dimensions of Those Decisions?

I have difficulty pointing to a particular decision or action and deciding whether it is Christian or not. I think the reason for this is that Christianity has two important concerns: (1) the relation of God to man such as that implied in the first Great Commandment, and (2) the relation of man to man such as that implied in the second Great Commandment.

As for the first concern—being saved, life after death, the heavenly reward, etc.—I believe that traditional Christianity, which I have been taught, has oversimplified these great mysteries. I cannot believe that a simple, one-time act, utterance, or ritual will ensure being "saved" after death; I cannot believe that conditions leading to unhappiness in this world will ensure happiness in the next; I cannot believe that denying my own well-being (as I understand it) for the well-being of others (as I understand it) will lead to any particular rewards after death.

Rather, if there is any spiritual survival after death for me, I feel that it is more likely related to actions through which I promote "heaven on earth," which require a lifetime of living for accomplishment.

This, then, suggests actions involving the relations with my fellowmen. These fill my life. I certainly can find no security or hope for eternal life merely by my actions in church one or two hours each week; surely, my goals and behavior all day long every day are my main opportunity to promote happiness for myself and others. This includes the actions of my business decisions.

Consider the previously described case of the assistant. The first job is to acquaint the man with the nature of the change, in this case from almost full-time safety director to half-time safety director and half-time educational assistant. This kind of change amounts to a change in the basic employment agreement between the company and the man. Like all agreements, this change cannot be made unilaterally. I think a wise company would not make such a decision and announce to the man that effective on such and such a day his new job will be thus and so.

Does he agree with such a change? He must be given the chance to know the reasons, to explore the implications, to examine the alternatives. Frequently my action is modified or completely changed as a result of the creative interchange between the assistant and me.

In this case, the assistant saw the action as a challenge for him to move into new fields in which he had an interest.

The second thing we did was to revise the position guide describing the new job. He wrote the new guide and I reviewed with him certain points, modified some, added a few. In each case we agreed to the changes. Again, he and I were self-determining within the framework of company goals to which both of us are committed, as evidenced by the fact that we both choose to work for *this* organization among thousands of others.

The next thing we did together was to write down a list of achievement goals. I do not believe that I can or should "motivate" my assistant to do a job. This would be manipulative. Nor should I motivate him toward depriving himself of something he may like for himself (like money) in order to get him to do something he doesn't like for somebody else (such as work).

But when my assistant participates in designing his own job and in setting his own achievement goals for something he wants as well as something the company wants, then his work is his own. I do not try to motivate him to achieve; rather, I provide an opportunity for achievement so that the achievement itself will motivate.

As manager, I do not try to work on my men to try to

change them; I work on the jobs, the work environment, and on myself to create the conditions and opportunity for achievement so that the people in my department can grow.

I'm not sure whether the principles of company identification, agreement, self-determination, goal setting, achievement, and creative action are Christian or not. Biblical history does not stress these words. They are modern words if not modern concepts. But I believe they are important for human happiness.

There are several other moral dimensions to my job. My words must be consistent with my actions, otherwise I cannot be trusted. As long as I personally identify with the goals of my company, I must faithfully represent these interests in reaching agreements with people who work in my organization. Any employee can choose to break the employment agreement by quitting, and I have the right, in representing the company, to discharge an employee when agreements regarding achievement cannot be reached. The discharged employee, in all probability, can identify better with some other organization.

I respect competence, because it is the result of a history of achievement of worthwhile goals. I believe that freedom and differences are essential if respect for the individual is to have any meaning at all. I also believe that order and certain kinds of conformity are essential if cooperation and community are to have any meaning at all. The tension created by these apparently opposite values is also essential for human growth, because this tension created by the dual necessity for freedom and order leads to interactions, negotiations, and agreements which is a creative process, and this is the way people grow. By way of analogy, the conditions for growth and creativity are found through the interaction of unlike elements; the hot sun and the cool earth give rise to life; positive and negative ions interact in chemical reactions; male and female interact in biological creativity; the warm air close to the cool damp earth is a condition for plant growth.

In my business decisions, I usually am faced with a situation in which opposing interests are present. Our salesman wants to set a low price; our treasurer wants to set a high price. I must help them to agree to a right price. My assistant wants to do many things himself; I try to persuade him to delegate more to other men, so that he himself can be more useful to the company and also create opportunities for his men to grow.

My motives in making decisions on my job tend to (1) promote the growth of my company; (2) promote the growth of each employee within the company; (3) satisfy the needs or interests of those outside the company; and (4) promote my own growth.

I find it possible to make decisions which do all these things. If these are not Christian dimensions of decision making, then Christianity has little to say to me about my business decisions.

But I believe they are.

What Do I Consider to Be the Major Resources Available to Me as I Make the Decisions My Job Requires?

I interpret "resources" to mean those people and things I draw upon in making decisions.

Of course, I accept the responsibility for the decisions I make. In doing so, I also accept the risks entailed in every decision. In order to help minimize these risks, I need to acquire as many facts related to the decision as I can gather in the time I have available. This means trying to perceive reality as best I can.

The resources I draw upon in making decisions are related to the four ends toward which my actions are directed and which were listed in the previous section. If the decision is to better promote the growth of my company, I need to know as much as possible about the policies, goals, and objectives of the company.

For this information I look mainly to the man to whom I report, and to other leaders of the company. Published material about the company, such as annual reports, is helpful.

If my decisions are to promote the growth of each employee within the company, then I must be careful to perceive accurately the interests of those employees affected by the decision. If only one or a few employees are affected, it is simply necessary to interview these employees before making the decision; sometimes the decision is modified as a result of such interviews. When hundreds or thousands of em-

57

ployees are affected by the decision, the risk is greater but may be reduced by conferring with a number of managers (who may in turn make spot checks with some employees). Employee attitude surveys are helpful to maintain accurate perceptions about what employees want.

If a decision is to satisfy the needs or interests of those outside the company, such as customers, vendors, or stockholders, the same perception of interests is necessary. I personally do not make many marketing, procurement, or financing decisions. But if I did, I would try to stay as sensitive as possible to the interests and express needs of customers, vendors, and stockholders.

If my decisions are to promote my own growth, I have the most difficult facts of all to perceive. What are my strengths and my limitations? My strengths have surely been built from many resources: my parents, my teachers, my friends, my wife, my managers—in fact, all the people I have ever met have contributed to my strengths. A few, undoubtedly, have contributed to my weaknesses; but I suspect most of my weaknesses have been my own doing.

But perceiving as many facts about a problem as possible in order to make a good decision is not enough. Facts pertain to the past and the present; where do you get "facts" about the future? Yet, the most important aspects of most decisions relate to the future, because the decision changes the past into the future—converts the "is" into the "will be"—changes a hope into reality. The most essential ingredients of my decision making, beyond the acquisition of facts, are my personal estimates about the future and what it might be. These estimates are loaded with problems of risk, of hope, of faith, of trust, of responsibility, of confidence.

How do I acquire or maintain these attitudes? By a simple faith that they are right. I place confidence in a man, and my expectations are fulfilled more often than not; I assume responsibility for myself and others and am honored for doing so more often than not; I trust a man even though I may have doubts, and my expectations are rewarded more often than not; I have confidence in myself and others, because I could not be happy in a world in which I could not have confidence; I maintain hope, for this is the wellspring of the excitement in decision making; I willingly accept the risk in all these expectations, because when my positive assumptions are correct the decision is successful; when I am wrong, I can usually find ways of retrieving a bad situation, modifying the decision, exploring reasons for failure, and thereby learn a lesson, or simply chalk it up as a miss. If that did not occasionally happen, there would be no risk in decision making, decisions would have no challenge, and I would have little opportunity to grow.

Other aids also help. Respectful listening, asking discerning questions, quiet periods, thought, meditation, privacy —all are worthwhile to me. This is my concept of prayer.

In describing these resources for decision making, I have not mentioned God as resource. I could have said, "God is my resource" which would have included all the things I have said. But in making such a brief statement the reader would not have known my own unique perception and understanding. I have tried to describe the only kind of God I know in the way he works through me; this is my idea of a personal God. The behavior and attitudes I have described are my idea of love. I have no other.

MORAL DILEMMAS IN THE
WIELDING OF WORDS   *Carroll Thompson*

My livelihood is mass communications. I own and operate
a small public relations firm in which our work is to help
people in business, industry, associations, and institutions
to tell their story to those they wish to impress with a
distinct message.

It is an important service work and offers a kaleidoscopic
experience potentially as broad as living itself. Therefore,
it offers the same broad range of opportunities for Christian commitment. To say that I have been able to apply
Christian standards as fully as I ought would be the kind

of a boastful statement I will not make. I have sought to be guided by the Christian concept and to make decisions according to it. Several years of experience have taught me that it is a field that offers great opportunity for application of Christian thought and ethics. It should be a field of continuing concern for Christians.

My firm operates with the conviction that every person and every firm or group has a right and an obligation to describe its purpose for being, its services or products, and the benefits it believes it is bringing or can bring to an individual and society.

It is obvious that we may not in all cases agree with the ideas or information we are asked to communicate. Neither can we dictate conditions to weave what we believe to be Christian thought and Christian action into every message or every action with which we are concerned.

We try to be as a signpost, directing the way we believe work should be done.

For us to judge every message of every client, and to reject or accept it for communication, would be presumptuous. We do not have the information sufficient to pass judgment on every product, every piece of information, with which we are asked to work. But we can work only with people whom we believe to be upright in their purposes. This we seek to do. We fail and we succeed. We seek to look at everything with an unprejudiced eye. But we know we cannot do that. We are imperfect, but we do not disdain perfection.

Let's consider some examples of the kind of decisions one must make in the communications field.

Politics is a dangerous game, especially for those in the advertising and public relations business who cast their lot with a losing candidate or a losing cause. Such losses can measurably affect your business. But even the most obscure candidate for the most obscure office usually wants the help of a professional advertising and public relations firm. The weakest cause will seek to strengthen its voice through professional advertising and public relations.

In the early years of the business we worked for many unpopular causes and for minor candidates. This occurred because we were a new firm seeking to make its way in a community where most of the fatter clients were long married to other good firms. Thus the smaller ones tended to come to us. As a result we worked for Democratic candidates in a Republican-dominated area, when the fact was that Democratic candidates had virtually no one else to go to for help. We worked for causes which were too controversial for others. We conducted local campaigns for urban renewal, for fluoridation, and for other public issues in elections. We conducted campaigns for statewide issues. We won some and we lost some. We were unpopular with some factions for working with certain causes or with certain candidates. We were berated by those who disagreed with the cause or the candidate, and we were applauded by those who supported them.

But the key factor in all this work was that we always tried to present information in perspective. We sought to deaden rumors not based on fact, to highlight objective information which a voter could hang onto and reason with. Sometimes, too late, we found we were not working with facts ourselves. In our zeal we would not always present the material objectively.

I have come to recognize that those who work in mass communications are to a startling degree frontline troops in the battle of ethical practice. They may exercise great control over what thousands of people believe about topics with which they work. Their decisions about what to put into news stories, into advertising copy, and into their recommendations for group action may affect their community or state for years to come. Deciding, often on the spur of a moment, how to perform your task can have great social significance.

A state tax issue my firm is now involved in promoting is a good example. I have been personally involved for a number of years in seeking a broadened tax base for our state. I have also worked as a volunteer in a statewide citizens group to seek to save a state income tax law, recently enacted, which is being challenged through public referendum at an upcoming election. Our group sought to have the referendum drive declared void in court, but we lost in the State Supreme Court. I feel the court erred in judgment but have accepted the decision as being arrived at in good faith.

Now the issue is before the people in a statewide election. The group I am associated with sought for months, through an education program, to have the public inform itself on the matter. We feel they have not done so. Apathy is rampant. The court has decided against us. The decision is now before the people and we feel they have not used the opportunity for education offered them. Yet they will make the decision to retain or discard the law.

As a result, the people in our organization decided to take the funds that were left in the organization treasury and invest them in an advertising campaign. I was asked to handle the advertising and to suggest an approach. My suggestion was that under the conditions we use our brief advertising messages to direct the people, rather than to educate them, as we had tried to do in the past. I suggested this tactic, realizing it is not the most desirable route. My preference would be to have time to reach each voter, to offer him the opportunity for full give-and-take discussion on the issue of his vote. Through those means, I am certain, we could attain the end we seek. But a shortcut is necessary.

Therefore my firm is using its best talent to tell voters only part of the story and to make the straight command, which is key to virtually all advertising. We are saying only, "Vote for . . . ," and dramatizing all the best reasons we can, tying them to the personal interest of a cross section of the population.

When I apply ethical judgment to this decision, I realize it is questionable. But certainly the opponents have forced our hand. And, most important of all, we firmly believe that what we recommend is right, even if our method lacks the best ethics. In the end the best interests of the people will be served, we believe.

Today we accept little political business, however. It upsets the schedule of service to regular clients. It's just not good business for us. But we have not closed the door on it, because we feel a responsibility to help when other work does not take our time.

We made the decision long ago that we would not turn down any political issue just because it was unpopular, or just because the candidate was of a party different from our own. We have stuck with that decision and will continue to do so. There are other firms like mine who have decided to work only with Republican candidates, for example. Possibly they have prospered more this way. I haven't examined their books. I do examine my conscience quite often. Every time I do I'm more convinced than ever that I have to keep the door open. No one is all wrong or all right.

There are many other decisions one must make which are related to one's religion.

For example, I am a Lutheran. I work with institutions in public relations. Do I work solely for Lutheran, or Protestant, institutions? My answer has been "no." Today we serve one Lutheran institution and one which is Roman Catholic. We serve one which is supported by all faiths. We haven't done this in an attempt to be all things to all people. We do it because their needs have come to our attention and we felt we had the services they needed. This is one very basic decision and not one for which we claim merit. This is the least that someone in this work must do.

Two examples of problems regarding one client may find wide identification. The Lutheran nursing home we work with has a good reputation and has served its area well.

We advise them in general public relations and fund raising, as well as performing informational work. This home is supported by a synod which has to support far more institutions than others of its size. Eventually, this nursing home will have to gain an increasing percentage of its benevolent support from the community in which it is located. Therefore we have advised them to retain the strong identification as a Christian home, but to plan for more community financial support. To gain this added community support, it must identify itself to the business and industry community to a greater extent than ever before. In doing this, it comes into direct contact with a Roman Catholic institution in the community which virtually duplicates its service.

Both institutions are planning a community fund-raising effort. After long consideration of their situations, I recommended as strongly as I could that they unite in a single community fund-raising effort. My feeling is that both institutions will get more money and more lasting support in this way. This is the case because our community has adopted the "community unit plan" for hospital giving, in which all hospitals go together in one fund effort. I argued that business firms would be put in a painful quandary should both homes seek funds in separate fund efforts within a year or two as they had planned.

My recommendation is being explored and will probably be carried forward. Many of my own church people do not agree with this method. But I have faith that it will prove to be the best road.

Another case in point for this same nursing home involved

the material for a quarterly bulletin insert for congregations of the synod. With so much government programming for nursing homes today, there is widespread discussion about the need for the Christian nursing home. Many church institutions have chosen to ignore this honest questioning of lay people and the clergy. I favor a full "on-the-table" discussion of it, because I am convinced that such discussion will strengthen the church institutions. So we recommended that the bulletin insert copy ask the direct question, "Why a church-supported, Christian home, when all the government programs are available?" We are producing the bulletin on this plan and believe it is not only the best thing to do, but action that is following the Christian ethic.

A key decision in our work is how to invest the talents of yourself and your employees. What do you want those talents to do for people? Since my business is a corporation and I direct it, I make this decision. Do we want to sell aspirin, automobiles, soap, beer, bank services, furniture, fire alarms, or windows? Do we want to sell causes or philosophies? Is one line a Christian one and the other not?

To me there is no line that can be drawn. I cannot accept or reject one over the other. How, then, do I choose? Here is the basis I use, and my reasoning for it. I believe that the gospel of Jesus Christ calls each of us to work on the task of completing God's creation. I cannot believe that the creation was a completed job which a loving God would perform, dust off his hands, and sit back to watch over it all. Creation is an ongoing work. It will be completed only when man has closed the gap and made himself and his society as perfect and as just as it can be. It is never ending.

As a child of God my ministry is to be a creator. My work is my ministry. I have this vast, open-ended assignment which in my lifetime I can never hope to complete. But it is not in the completion that I find myself and my rightful place with God. It is in the attempt.

Each of us has only so much time, talent, and energy to invest in his work. We are called on every day to make choices about how we make that investment. The fact that we choose to work for a political candidate rather than doing advertising for a soap company does not mean that the soap account is less Christian, or unchristian, compared to the political campaign. Nor does it mean the political account is more Christian. It simply means that, at the time I made the choice, I felt it was more important for me to do the one and let the other be done by someone else. I do not make the final, fearful judgment that one task is all Christian and the other all non-Christian. I use a moral slide rule. This does not rob me of any of the tools I have to make judgments. I try to make it tell me at what place and in what way I can do my best.

A benevolent teacher of college physics helped me learn this lesson at Carthage College, where I received my undergraduate training. Obviously out of my element in the class, I was not doing well and did not really care to do well. During the final examination he came to my desk and asked me what I wanted to do in life. I told him that I was not certain, but since I loved to write and had achieved some minor recognition for my writing, I felt I should do something in that field. He graciously gave me a passing grade without comment. His act was more powerful than a sermon. From then on I concentrated in communications and have never been sorry for it.

Luther hit hard on this same point. Do what you do best and honor your work, he said. This direction has helped me reach deeply into the possibilities in communications and allowed me to do what I feel I can do best.

To me there is a natural extension to it. Do what you do best, do what you feel compelled to do, and do not do something which you feel saps your time and talent from your true ministry of work. There is a right choice in each decision, and you are obligated to seek that right choice. If you feel you are contributing most by selling soap, sell soap. If you don't like to sell soap and would rather sell something else, sell something else.

When you own and operate a personal business, as I do, you can make the decisions to a much finer point than many employed people. Before I had my own business, I felt unfulfilled. I felt I was cheating myself. And if I cheated myself, I cheated God. I worked, for instance, as a professional fund raiser. My job was to supervise the "communications" work, or the public relations phase of campaigns. After eighteen months at it, I could not bring myself to agree with the ethics of the firm and my superiors. I resigned as quickly as I was able. I founded my own business and thus was able to set my own standards. This, too, was a step toward fulfillment, toward greater realization of the aim to do what I could do best, to do what I felt compelled

70

to do, and to do something that I felt was not distracting me from my ministry of work.

Excellence is a word that has guided me. Not that I presume all I do is excellent. It is not. We turn out some sloppy work. We turn out work that is not as good as it could have been for the client. But we operate with the idea that we must seek excellence in our work, and that we must cultivate an appreciation of excellence in our clients.

Recently we produced two brochures which illustrate two important points regarding excellence. One was a small, rather obscure piece of work which we had tried to make outstanding. The printer did not follow our directions, and the product was mediocre at best. But the client was immeasurably pleased with it. The client felt it was a wonderful job and said so profusely. I took time to point out to the client why we felt it was a failure. And I took the blame. All of the cause for mediocrity was not with the printer. Some of it was mine. I felt compelled to tell my client this and did so. The client was undisturbed. But I feel we made a point that will serve us well in getting him to require better work in later assignments.

In another case, we recommended a printing job that was more expensive and beyond the needs the client saw. We stressed that we wanted to produce a printed piece that would be as excellent as we could make it. We argued that excellence always has merit, and that it always does more for the dollar invested than a mediocre job. The client accepted our arguments and agreed to invest twice as much money in the job as he had intended. We devoted more time and effort per dollar of income to the job than if we had tried for only a mediocre product. The result was what we felt to be an outstanding piece of work. It has been praised by professional people and lay people alike. It brought interest in the information from sources we never knew would be interested. The pattern of it is being copied. The client has recognized the validity of our original arguments and now depends on us more and more.

We believe in excellence and we feel we achieved it with this one effort. "The best-kept secret in America today is that people would rather work hard for something they believe in than enjoy a pampered idleness," John W. Gardner has written. To believe in excellence is not enough. We have to stand up for it even when the man who pays the bill wants you to settle for less. Be firm but not unreasonable. But make sure you definitely feel that it is for his own good that you seek excellence. Make the case for excellence, believe in it, work for it. Yet recognize that it, too, must win its way by persuasion.

The hardest decisions in my work concern a client's specific needs. Since many of the people we work with trust us as "the experts," they gladly plunge into recommendations we make. Responsibility weighs heavily on us. We have no large national advertising accounts, for instance, so we are not making decisions regarding how to spend millions of dollars. But if we were, the ground rules would be the same. A thousand dollars to a small client may be more critical than a million to another. The problem is to take the client, his work, aims, and situation into perspective.

Begin working with him where he is today, not where he hopes to be tomorrow. Try to make sure that every dollar you spend for him will advance him toward his goal. Try to make sure that what you recommend in the way of advertising or PR is within a sensible budget. Make sure he understands exactly what his costs will be and exactly what he gets for his money. This is a part of the process of educating him to what he must do to reach the goals you set with him.

In our work we are in contact with clients when they are at the height of tension in many cases. We are in daily contact with people in the news media, artists, printers, promotion people. The urgency to act without all the facts at hand, or to make snap judgments, is ever before us. Keeping ourselves organized is a must. We also work hard to keep our clients organized. But in the end, we shoulder the blame for any disorganization because I feel it is a requirement of the productive person that he carry forward his work with planned deliberateness, that he not rush. Fast work is necessary, but behind the flying fingers at the typewriter we try to keep a calm head and to keep others calm and organized.

The book of Genesis tells us that God reduces chaos to order. This is a part of the creative task. As creative people working to push forward the creation of a society under God, we are called to be organized, to work calmly from plan. In our work we do this by helping people correctly organize their problems.

The temptation to let yourself be hired to do what you cannot do well has been one of the major problems I have faced. To the person outside the profession, public relations and advertising are all one and the same. A copywriter in a radio station is an expert in PR. An announcer can conduct public opinion polls. An advertising salesman can organize a productive group meeting. A newspaperman can outline and execute a public relations program for an institution. A printer is a direct-mail expert. These are some of the misconceptions many people have. Quite understandably they do not see that within our profession there are specialists who can do only a few things well.

As a firm we are often called on to do work we are not professionally equipped to do. A client wants a public opinion poll conducted. A client wants a layout artist to paint a point-of-sale sign. Since we write newspaper and magazine articles, we are asked to write a movie script.

We consistently turn these down. We do it for professional reasons and for moral reasons. Since we don't do these things well, we hire outside suppliers to do them for us. But we explain to clients that we do not do them. So a part of our work is to emphasize what we cannot do, as well as what we can do. This has caused us temporarily to lose income in many cases. But to have taken the money for work we did not feel competent in doing would have been taking it under false pretenses.

James A. Pike has written that a man should try to bring "judgment and grace into every situation so far as he may," in his vocation. I shy away from the term grace. I cannot assume to exercise it. What I can try to do is to go through my workday with a sense of deep conviction about how my job must be done; about the relative importance of doing it consciously as a part of God's creative process; and about the negation I have strewn about when it is done otherwise.

Much of what Karl Barth said in a BBC address in regard to the church, I would like to say also. I do say it to clients who will understand. I should say it to many business associates. I should like to say it to those who have messages that are welling up inside them. Barth said this:

"Why are you not saying what you ought to say and saying it with power and eloquence? Why don't you force us to pay attention to you and listen to you? We should like to see you less timid, more consistent, bolder. We often have the impression you are afraid—of what, really?"

The interesting thing about this statement to me is that the entire object of his challenge is better communications. He pleads for straight-from-the-shoulder communications. I am intrigued by the power that words wield. I know that where the mighty army of God marches, strong words go on before. I know that when strong words go on before— when strangers understand us fully, when friends really know what we mean—there is less bloodshed, less turmoil, less time wasted in hatred. For words lead to understanding, and understanding stamps out hatred.

Today's life is a bracing experience, not so much because of the chances we have to live fully and to help others live fully; but because of the teeming future of man under God. I shudder when I think of the tremendous changes which will take place in communications—of the speed with which we can tell one another what we know. The revolution is moving about us like a thunderstorm. Today we sit in our living room and listen to a man talk as he walks in space. Block-long presses turn out hundreds of thousands of newspapers a day. Radio signals millions of miles in space steer a rocket and activate a television camera. New drugs can help to open minds to allow the mentally ill to recognize and communicate their frustrations. Today man knows more, can tell people more, than at any time in history.

The wonders of this revolution are common coin to Americans, and to millions in other countries. We are living through an atomic explosion in communications. Libraries of today will be replaced by data banks which can be activated by radio signals and bounced off satellites by people thousands of miles away.

It is indeed an astounding future we face in communications. Thus the temptation to misuse techniques will increase. Christians must work just as hard to develop their abilities to use these techniques ethically as scientists have worked to originate them. The more sophisticated the system becomes, the greater the opportunity for misuse.

For example, plagiarism was not a real social problem until the invention of the printing press. Thought control was not a problem until the machines became available to make thought control possible. Today those machines are in everyday use. In spite of watchful government control of news media, it is still possible for one advertiser to saturate a market with the message he wants to promote. He can do it with a bigger budget. He can do it with better production or materials. He can do it, in some cases, by buying up all available media space. For example, there are only so many billboards available at one time in a community; or so many bus-card showings. If one advertiser dominates any one of these, he may gain an advantage he ought not to have.

A Christian ought to exert Christian ethical consideration in these matters. If he does, great good can be worked with the wonders we have created.

It is a wondrous age for the Christian to behold. How Paul, floating on a battered raft, would have used even the simplest of our modern instruments of communications is exciting to reflect upon. How we, with what we know must be communicated, will use them is breathtaking to consider.

A LABOR LEADER DISPELS
SOME STEREOTYPES   *Dallas Sells*

One of the most difficult tasks a labor leader has in interpreting his job is to overcome the stereotyped image promoted by the mass media and the implication that all labor leaders have the same tasks and operate by the same code of ethics.

This should be easy to dispel, but unfortunately the conditioning of thought along this line has been rather successful. It is somewhat like the false impressions that "blondes have more fun," or "redheads are naturally more argumentative."

When one tries to define "Christian Decisions," he immediately runs into the question of whether there are Christian actions or merely Christians acting in the involvements of life. Despite this hazard, I believe some general comment can be made concerning the three propositions raised: What is your job and what does it mean to you? What are the kinds of decisions your job requires you to make? What do you consider to be the Christian dimensions of those decisions?

In 1954 I was elected president of the Indiana Congress of Industrial Organizations (CIO) by delegates to a state convention on a representative basis, representing the various local unions affiliated with our organization. At the merger convention of the Indiana Federation of Labor (AFL) and the Indiana CIO, I was elected president and have been reelected at conventions held biennially since that time.

A state labor organization acts as a coordinating body for the various international unions in a number of fields. In Indiana we have four elective officers, four staff members, six secretaries, and one custodian.

Obviously my first task is one of administration. Operating an organization with an affiliation of approximately 350,000 members representing some 1400 local unions and 60 international unions requires time and patience. Securing affiliation of the various local unions and understanding the different policies of each of the sixty or more international unions requires a measure of diplomacy and patience not generally needed in a business venture of similar magnitude because of the autocratic nature of the business community. The necessity of finding a "consensus" compatible with certain ethical standards is sometimes difficult, never impossible.

Our first major responsibility is that of being the legislative representative for Indiana AFL-CIO. This responsibility means a great deal more than the term generally implies. Our organization must become informed about legislative matters in all fields, as almost all legislation affects our membership in one way or another. We cannot confine our interests to what is generally considered to be in "labor's legitimate area of concern," meaning wages, hours, and working conditions.

It is imperative, therefore, to understand state and local financing, taxation, and expenditures. There are basic decisions in this area that some consider Christian in nature. For example, should consideration in taxation only deal with the economic needs of the state, or should you also consider the impact of taxes on those least able to pay? In 1963, after a deadlock in the regular session of the Indiana General Assembly and a special session, the taxpayers were faced with a new tax system that included a sales tax. Our organization took the legislation to court because of constitutional questions, and because the tax burden was shifted from those most able to pay to those least able to pay. The case went to the U.S. Supreme Court and, while part of the battle was won, the major portion of the new tax structure remains to this day.

We are vitally concerned with problems of mental health, education, welfare, etc. Each of these fields finds Christian laymen on both sides of specific issues. For example, one of the controversial issues in Indiana is the question of abolition of capital punishment, for we still use the electric chair as the "ultimate penalty."

In each session the question of pari-mutuel betting becomes more and more controversial.

On the question of the so-called (but misnamed) "right-to-work" law, passed in 1957 and repealed in 1965, clergymen testified both for and against the issue.

These are just a very few of the many, many issues in which you can find sincere Christians disagreeing as to what the "Christian position" ought to be.

On legislative programs the tactics and mechanics are as much a part of decision making as the issues. Some of the problems raised in this area have been solved from a practical point of view while one might, on occasion, question the ethics involved.

Some organizations use "hospitality rooms" as a device to influence legislators. (Free liquor, beer, and sandwiches are available anytime day or night.) Some organizations pay the hotel room bill of important legislative leaders. Others may use the offer of specific job opportunities. Labor in Indiana uses none of these methods, but, in general, we use the power of the ballot box to encourage legislators to "see our position." Are these methods ethical? I can only say that the nature of our society makes these programs common to our legislative system. I am sure everyone is aware of these and other practices. The Indiana Council of Churches has its legislative representatives actively supporting the causes as they see them.

One of the major tasks of legislative representatives is to serve on various legislative advisory commissions and committees. Most of our officers and staff have been appointed to one or more committees. These committees and commissions deal with taxes, mental health, education, good government, our judicial system, election codes, etc.

Here again the responsibility of obtaining accurate facts and reaching the best decisions is a very complex one. Yet the multitude of meetings thus required as well as the research necessary are part of the duty of our office.

The pressure of various groups is sometimes so great that a decision becomes problematic: When is it consensus and when is it a surrender of basic ideas and principles? As someone once stated, "Politics is the art of the possible." Who among us mortal men can stand and say without fear of failure: Here is the Christian answer?

It seems obvious to most of us that legislation is really enacted on election day. This is true because most elected officials are fairly well conditioned by their economic, social, and educational environment. In Indiana, for example, it was until recently fashionable to be opposed to "federal aid" as something subversive. This opposition developed even though it is quite evident that Hoosiers were paying "double taxes" for many projects. It was so ridiculous that a former governor, when asked to apply for $130,000 to supply mobile library units to rural counties, refused on the grounds that he did not want "federal bureaucrats brainwashing Hoosier farmers"!

Labor became politically active not because they wanted

to, but because employer groups were very effective in denying at the legislative table what they granted at the bargaining table.

The myth that labor is all powerful at the ballot box and controls the various state assemblies and Congress can be exposed on simple examination. With all the progressive legislation being passed by the 1966 Congress—medicare, civil rights, aid to education, etc.—the four primary "labor measures" have met a sad fate. The federal minimum wage and unemployment compensation bills are a mere shadow of the original proposals. The repeal of Section 14 B and the restriction of the meaning of a secondary boycott are still in committee. In Indiana it took nine years to repeal the so-called "right-to-work" law. While we admit Christian laymen are found on both sides of such issues, the facts clearly show that labor is not all powerful politically.

There are no areas more divisive to our organization than politics, the position on issues, and the selection of the best candidates to support. Yet this is the responsibility of our state organization. On the question of issues, our position is determined by the passage of resolutions at our convention. Naturally there are various shades of opinions on most issues, and we operate by majority rule.

Just as Christian organizations are not in agreement on such issues as Vietnam, Civil Rights, etc., so we are divided. The entire question involved, it would seem to me, would be whether decisions made in this area are "Christian decisions" or whether Christians make decisions. It makes a real difference which of the answers you as a layman regard as the proper one.

On the question as to who might be the better candidate, the differences of opinion are equally great. Some of our members are either Democrat or Republican, first and above all else. Others, of course, look at the individual, not the label. Indiana AFL-CIO uses a democratic method: Our members who live in the geographical area from which the candidate is running make the decision as to endorsement and support. Even so there is still a difference of opinion. Our organization is responsible for coordinating, insofar as possible, the political activities of our affiliates. We provide them with copies of the platforms of both major parties, voting records and positions on issues. We encourage programs designed to get the maximum number of citizens registered and voted on election day. Yet there are some Christians I know who refuse to vote since voting is "worldly." Others tell me: "You can't be a Christian and be in politics. Politics is a dirty business. All politicians are crooked." This is so obviously untrue that to answer is to dignify a real lack of understanding of our democratic system. As Vice-President Humphrey once said, while he was still a United States Senator, "Politics is the practical housekeeping business of our great nation, and if the citizens fail to tend to this business they will get the business." How can Christians expect to find "Christian solutions" to the political problems of our society by refusing to participate? This only leaves the decisions to non-Christians.

Thus one finds in the legislative and political areas of

responsibility, insofar as the Indiana AFL-CIO is concerned, questions and problems demanding decisions almost daily in which Christians can sincerely differ. I believe one can genuinely hope, however, that the more Christian laymen participate, the greater the chance of a better solution to the problems facing every individual on this globe of ours.

Another area of responsibility I have, as president of the Indiana AFL-CIO, is to coordinate educational activities of our affiliates. This is a very important area, because far too often the program has been indoctrination rather than education. Our goal is to see that our society provides equal opportunity for all Americans to achieve their maximum potential without artificial barriers (economic or social).

This goal means we must fight in the halls of the general assembly for enough tax dollars to provide this opportunity. We must make every effort to see that these tax dollars are raised in the most equitable method. We must help resolve the problems of both secondary and post-high school education. There is, of course, a continuous fight to see that educators are free to educate rather than forced to indoctrinate. In Indiana, if you exclude the monetary problem, the educational debates will concern the question of the advisability of a board of regents over the state universities, establishment of junior colleges or regional vocational institutes, etc. Labor must play an important part in this decision-making process. Our officers and staff serve on various school organizations as trustees and advisors; they work with legislative committees and trust that the final decisions are just. Sometimes the decision-making process is very difficult, as we are amateurs dealing with professionals. For example, a very controversial issue in Indiana is: Should the Indiana University Medical School in Indianapolis be expanded, or is it too large, or should a new medical school be located elsewhere in the state? Our organization will be expected to support one or the other proposition. A decision will have to be made.

Today with the federal government becoming more and more involved in education, the problem is one of degree. How far should the federal government be permitted to intrude on "states' rights" in education? How effective are the Job Corps, Pre-School, Vocational-Technical Programs now established?

Yes, in the field of education there are a great number of decisions our society will make. Indiana AFL-CIO will have a part to play in those decisions. We can only hope our position will be just and fair to all concerned.

Another major area in which the Indiana AFL-CIO is concerned is that of Community Services. Here we provide programs designed to help our membership and the general public become aware of the public and private agencies associated with the United Funds, unmet needs of their community, and state and federal services available to our local communities.

As in the other areas mentioned, Christian laymen have differences of opinion as to the merits of social legislation pertaining to public agencies. The philosophy of our organization is that we should give those citizens more unfortunate than ourselves a "handup" rather than a handout. This is not to say that we would resist the temporary assistance so often needed. In fact, quite the contrary is the case.

In this area both legislation and education are of vital importance. In 1963, there was a debate over a bill that would raise the amount paid under the Aid to Dependent Children Act to a mother with one child from $80 to $100 per month. The chairman of the House Ways and Means Committee stated publicly that the amount was more than enough and should not be raised! Thus what seems to be obvious to many of us becomes a legislative and political issue to others.

Another responsibility of my job is to further the cause of civil rights which means equal treatment and opportunity for all.

This is a difficult task, since within the house of labor there are still those who resist. Discrimination does exist in our society. We need to understand, as Victor Hugo said, "There is nothing more powerful than an idea whose time has come." The idea of social revolution is upon us. We can pretend that it does not exist and have violence and disorder, or we can, as reasonable men, face the issue.

Through legislation and education we strive to resolve the problems that cause brother to stand against brother. The time has come when we can no longer rearrange our prejudices but must face them fairly and squarely.

Yet the portion of truth in the statement that 11:00 o'clock each Sunday morning is the most segregated hour in America is sufficient to prove that Christians disagree even in this basic human relation. The clergy themselves are completely divided in this regard. There are those who support and those who deplore demonstrations, segregation, and integration.

Like it or not, the issue is upon us. Christians, who are said to be the moral leaders of our society, will have to make some difficult decisions, just as I have to in my job.

In addition to the above-mentioned responsibilities, we are required to cooperate with various administrative agencies. For example, I am presently serving on the Indiana Employment Security Board and the Advisory Board of the Indiana Department of Commerce.

On the Employment Security Board, decisions are faced concerning such items as at what point the benefits are such as to discourage workers from seeking other employment. This of course raises many ethical questions with Christian implication.

On the Department of Commerce Advisory Board questions arise with far-reaching implications such as, how far must we subsidize business in order to create new employment opportunities? How do you prevent plant piracy from other states? All are very complex problems demanding difficult decisions.

Thus it is easy to see that working with administrative agencies means dealing with many problems in which there are no simple solutions, and making decisions upon which Christian laymen might sincerely disagree.

Another area of responsibility is that of public relations—of interpreting to the general public and other organizations and groups the goals, aims, and aspirations of the Indiana AFL-CIO. This means being available at all times to the mass communication media. A newspaper that refuses to accept fully paid advertisements, to edit advertising, and to publish both sides of an issue is common occurrence in some areas. Yet an attempt must be made to secure proper publicity for our causes.

Speaking to educational classes at secondary and post-high school levels is a common obligation. Addressing service clubs, women's groups, church groups is also an essential part of my responsibility.

Another area of concern is finding job opportunities for those displaced because of plants moving or closing. There is presently a plant in Indianapolis in the process of closing which will result in 2600 employees being idled. The average age of these employees is forty-five; five hundred do not have a high school diploma; forty percent are Negroes. This means educational facilities need to be located, new skills need to be learned, and employers will have to relax employment standards so these taxpayers do not become tax consumers.

The question of relaxing apprenticeship standards is also an issue, since the usual limitation for entrance into such a program is eighteen to twenty-one years of age.

A consensus will have to be reached if opportunities for employment are to be found. The decisions will be difficult.

There are of course many other tasks that arise due to the total involvement of the Indiana AFL-CIO in the life of the community. While these are too numerous to mention, they are nonetheless equally important in the fulfilling of responsibilities resting upon those who work in the AFL-CIO councils throughout the nation.

My job means, then, a personal commitment to the problems of man, his interrelationships, his ambitions and dreams.

Such a job means facing controversy. One must be willing to stand alone on occasion, defending principles and issues against the group. It means being responsive to the wishes of the membership, yet always being in the lead in spite of the perils connected with involvement.

The question of the Christian dimensions of decision is far more difficult, because Christians differ as to those dimensions.

Too many of us fail to realize that the American Labor Movement feels it can gain its objectives through the existing political and economic systems of our society. Other labor movements throughout the world seek to change either the political or economic systems (or both) in which they are involved.

The American Labor Movement is essentially an economic and social organization. "Christian decisions" will only be made with the full participation of Christians in both management and labor.

The issues in labor-management relations are complex. There are very few simple answers to the problems dealing with the interrelationship of people. Only as Christians realize that they must be active in all phases of our society will Christianity truly become the leavening influence it ought to be. Man's inhumanity to man is well documented.

Christian compassion and concern has yet to make the impact it is capable of making. Each of us can make his influence felt in the occupation in which he is now engaged. Which way we go can mean the survival of mankind.

I believe it's worth the effort.

THE SUPPLY TRAINS
ARE MISSING   *Elliott Couden*

My chief business is real estate, but my company deals
also in insurance and auto licensing. These tasks present
serious ethical dilemmas as well as challenging experiences.
Most of my thirty-five years in the world of business have
been in the role of real estate broker. Our family owns and
operates its own business. We have three grown children
and have always been active in church relationships.

One of my competitors in business has been known to
observe, "You can't sell real estate with a Bible under your
arm." This is not pure cynicism, but I am convinced that its

essential implications are false. And as a Christian I welcome the opportunity to testify to that conviction from personal experience.

The real estate business presents many problems each day that must be placed under the lens of Christian ethics. For one thing it is a quasi-legal business. We must take examinations and be licensed by the state. Usually we belong to the Real Estate Board, which has a definite code of ethics and standards of practice. And we operate not only under rather rigid state laws but also under the regulations of multiple listing organizations in the community. In determining our fundamental business principles and in applying the various legal regulations to our actual business transactions, it is not always easy to be certain what is Christian.

In this office it is not enough that we work under established business procedures, such as the handling of monies, bookkeeping, legal documents, permanent records, and so forth. We must also keep in mind, all of us, that we have privileged information from our customers and that we enjoy in most cases the confidence of people who are making their largest life investments. What we say and do will have much influence upon their decisions. We are often cast in the role of personal guides bringing people together in contractual agreements and giving personal advice in many and diverse lines. This interpersonal character of our business requires not only good teamwork but also high quality of character in each member of the team, such as patience, empathy, and perceptiveness. Indeed, it calls for a degree of semi-professionalism, even though the members of the team do not have the training and discipline inherent in most professions.

Despite the great responsibilities and opportunities in this business, much of it is conducted by the exercise of personalities and persuasions, and not a little by the psychological exercises attendant on cupidity, status, and exclusiveness. It is a real temptation to let ego and desire become the central motivations in the purchase of a home. Too many buyers tend to stretch their buying and paying capacity to the maximum. Some real estate people sense this and look for the point of diminishing returns, even though it may be far from the buyer's best interest to have his reserve capacity reduced to minimal standards. Mortgage lenders often attempt to exercise some prudence in this area for the benefit of the borrower, but many buyers not only resist these limitations but engage in under-the-table deals in order to satisfy their desires, An experienced real estate operator recognizes these tendencies, and he approaches them with drooling lips or human compassion, depending upon his orientation. The seller often is looking for "a sucker" and takes the real estate salesman into his confidence. The basement may leak in the winter, the house may have many nonapparent defects, the neighbor may throw drunken brawls every Saturday night, but this fellow will tell the world that he has the best house in the best neighborhood. What should the salesman do when his principal sets up this standard of action?

Insurance is another branch of our business that demands difficult ethical decisions. The companies that use our services must depend upon honest underwriting at our level. But it would be possible for us to wink an eye at poor records in order to "get the business." In processing auto title transfers and selling license plates, we encounter blatant instances of fraudulent sales prices (to avoid the correct sales tax), forgery of documents, and many other deviations from honesty designed to avoid penalties, late charges, and so forth. Should we notarize a signature not made before us? Should we allow a date to be altered and close our eyes to it? Have we the courage to face the pressures and endure the recriminations that result from the practical application of a Christian conscience? Many times in our business we have to endure rejection by good friends, neighbors, and fellow church members who refuse to measure up to the underwriting requirements of auto insurance.

There are scores of similar dilemmas. One that faces us all today is the movement of racial minorities into hitherto all-white neighborhoods. Several chapters could be written on the attitudes of man toward man in the real estate field. What can a salesman do when he knows that the broker for whom he is working wants no part of racial housing activity? What can the broker do who is sensitive to his responsibility in this area but realizes that his salesmen are all bigoted?

In the fight of truth with falsehood we real estate people have recently been brought closer to the frontline trenches by the current bid of minority racial groups for freedom and equality. After much local agitation for action on the part of our city fathers, an open housing ordinance was recently prepared and, rather than responsible administrative action being taken, it was submitted to the voters for passage or rejection. The measure ultimately went down to defeat at the polls, but many felt that the educational opportunities provided were unprecedented. It also was a revelation of public and private attitude, motivation, and reservation.

Our office had adopted a policy of non-discrimination long before the problem received public prominence. The showing of dwellings to all financially qualified prospects resulted in an occasional sale to a minority buyer. When the issue exploded into the open, we found ourselves publicly and prominently identified as a rather rare species of businessmen, "with ethics deeply rooted in theological belief." Whether this was a valid rarity or not, it points directly to the thesis that after two thousand years of Christianity a simple public witness to justice and brotherhood can evoke almost incredulous reaction.

We also received a flow of mail that was preponderantly positive and supportive. But there was a malicious side, too. We experienced overt, anonymous telephone threats to put us out of business, or worse. Of greater significance, we found our office being subtly rejected by the community in which we primarily do our business. Our listings dropped off to a trickle. Some who had our "For Sale" signs displayed at their home had visitations from neighborhood delegations requesting a change of mind—and of real estate office! Friends, old customers, even fellow church members found it more convenient to take their business elsewhere—with some notable exceptions. We received a postgraduate course on how far most people will go to avoid identification with controversy of any kind. Our business status became so critical that I was almost forced off my "battle station." All our loyal and enlightened—and broke—salesmen were lost to us.

Obviously this economic attrition seemed to suggest that I renounce conviction and retire to the sidelines, alongside a majority of my silent fellow laymen. My three children, all in college, and my wife encouraged me to stay with it. I stayed with it. After the balloting was past, business gradually returned to normalcy.

During that hectic period I was also at odds with my trade association, the Real Estate Board, which led the fight against the city council's ordinance. I hear that there was much agitation to have me removed from the roster. Some of my fellow realtors, however, while not identifying themselves directly with my posture, made it clear that they would fight to maintain my right to speak my convictions without retribution. Besides, martyrs are tough on public relations!

Later, state legislation was proposed that would eliminate discriminatory practices in real estate offices. Again, I was eyeball to eyeball with my peers as we debated the issues before legislative committees at the state capitol. It was lonesome, but it was invigorating! We lost again, but shortly thereafter the real estate boards of the entire state, wary of public opinion and future legal forays in their direction, publicly adopted a code of practices that contained most of the elements of the violently opposed legislation!

Our business survived. Many in the ministry were deeply

concerned about our plight (including Jewish rabbis and Catholic priests), but there were no resources to back laity on the battle lines. It was as if a layman, encouraged to plant the symbol of the faith on top a snowcapped mountain, found himself there surrounded with lonely, howling winds and with no supply trains, little or no communication, and slim chance ever to return to the home base. I am not unhappy with any particular church for this deficiency. I am just aghast at the way the church prepares and supports its soldiers in battle! Maybe some of us had taken "Onward Christian Soldiers" a bit too literally.

During the campaign on open housing, I was invited to make public addresses on such topics as real estate and race, property values and race, the church and race, and so forth. Some of these invitations came from church groups, ministerial associations, and the like. While responding with gratitude to about seventy-five of these invitations in four or five months, I often wondered why there was so much hunger for basic information in these matters, and whether the church had been directing its vast resources for instruction along these lines. Many people, both inside and outside the church, were honestly seeking some valid, constructive way to express concern. But the churches were just not oriented to provide any significant programs with which these good people could become identified.

My "outside work" is mainly educational. I have helped set up seminars for Law Enforcement and the Community, a High School Conference on Human Relations (350 students from forty high schools, private, public, and parochial), and a Human Relations Conference for School Administrators. I have helped plan a lay conference, including a six-day inner-city study of urban problems, especially relating to poverty. There are other areas of responsibility such as president of the local Chamber of Commerce, commissioner on the Human Rights Commission, and member of the Department of Christian Life and Mission of the local Council of Churches.

Most of our employees and salesmen are not church-related. As a matter of fact, they often have an ill-concealed hostility toward the church. It is probably oversimplification, but I suspect that at the heart of this attitude lies a resentment toward the safe, smug, "Sunday-oriented" Christian. It is almost amusing that the essence of the church really lies within many who scorn its pretenses and institutions. We have had within our office some who appeared to have the hide of a rhino and yet were totally generous with time and energy when a customer needed real assistance. On such occasions I say that they are "the church in action," and though I may detect a rolling of eyeballs, they seem to give this observation some thoughtful consideration. They appear to enjoy working in an office that takes risks, and they especially enjoy the remarks from salesmen in other offices about the freedom that characterizes our organization.

Aside from the more strife-laden activities both inside and outside our office, I find opportunity for witness to be almost unlimited in everyday activities. Traffic is heavy in our office due to the many services offered. Consequently, many come to us with their personal problems, too. We must

99

stay within the limitations imposed by law and codes of ethics in attempting to give positive assistance to these people. Many have no minister and have little faith or trust in organized religion. But they do speak freely in what they term "a Christian office." We usually limit our help to lending a sympathetic ear. As a rule we observe ample release through the simple therapy of clarifying the problems whether real or imagined.

This is the world of business. We like it here. This is where people really live, where God lives. The world needs the good news of the fellowship. But it needs it in a way it has never heard before, in the language of the world, and related to the hopes and dreams and cares of the world.

AGENTS OF
TRANSFORMATION   *Jan J. Erteszek*

I am the head of a company engaged in the design, manufacture, and distribution of women's garments. We have three divisions, each producing a separate product category. We employ approximately six hundred people and have three plants located in various cities in California. My responsibilities do not differ greatly from those in similar positions concerned with the production and distribution of consumer goods. Like most American companies, ours is divided into the customary subdivisions of Manufacturing, Sales, Marketing, Advertising, Personnel, Design, and Finance. The heads of these divisions are responsible to me. I, in turn, am responsible for the determination of broad policy in these areas and for the formulation of long-range goals and objectives, which is accomplished with the assistance of our various department heads. Because we are a profit oriented organization, my further responsibility is to operate a business which is financially sound and which yields a profit. Inasmuch as we aspire to conduct a business in conformance with Christian principles, it is my further responsibility—in the selection of a product, an advertising campaign, or a personnel policy—to make certain that such selections and decisions be not only economically sound but morally valid. In addition, I must make certain that these goals are pursued in all our relationships—those with our customers, suppliers, competitors, and the ultimate consumer.

We are in a fashion business. The necessity to respond to the changing aesthetic preference of men and women gives our business a dimension which goes beyond the production and distribution of goods in which most manufacturing concerns are engaged. Part of my responsibility is to help in evaluating, responding, and sometimes creating new trends in fashion. As a Christian business, we try to see our response to fashion in broad and constructive terms. As garment makers, we feel this imposes upon us the responsibility of creating apparel which is technically and aesthetically superior, which fulfills the contemporary needs of people, and which is priced competitively. This, in turn, imposes upon the head of a company like ours specific responsibilities which make this job different, in many respects, from the job of an executive who deals with staple commodities or services. A business such as ours puts great emphasis on creativity. It makes it necessary to develop a climate in which the creative impulses of the men and women are generated, stimulated, and permitted to flow freely.

As the head of the company, it is also my responsibility to build an enterprise which is dynamic, competitive, sensitive to technology and change, capable of producing the growing volume needed to secure a satisfactory profit.

It is also my responsibility to plan for the future—in plant capacity, equipment, finance, and technology. At the present stage of our development, the human area is one to which I devote a substantial amount of my time and effort. There are both economic and broad moral considerations which justify my concentration on this area. An enterprise which tries to grow as an economic unit and also in its broad social influence must do it primarily through the development of its human resources.

I am charged with the selection of top managers. In this selection I must be sensitive to their professional competence and character as well as to the quality of their broad commitments. It is my responsibility to forge these managers into a purposeful team and, because of the kind of business we aspire to be or become, to make them, in turn, sensitive to human values in their own departments. Together with them, I must set long-range goals to help these men to develop to their utmost potential in competence, character, and purpose—to create a climate in which nothing is asked of them or by them which is alien to man—to permit them to develop to the utmost their own creative capabilities and provide for them the full freedom for individual effort consistent with the objectives of the company on the one hand, and a sense of belonging and fulfillment of their broad purposes on the other hand. In essence, I must create a climate in which our men and women are satisfied not only to make a living which is rewarding, but can find fulfillment to life itself.

Finally, I am responsible for the approval of all promotions and demotions, of disciplinary actions, and of the dismissal of those who are incompetent or whose work and actions are contrary to the broadest objectives and aspirations of the company.

I see my job as a means of making a living and supporting my family as well as providing for their future, and, equally, as a channel of the broadest exercise of the stewardship of life, for this is the place where I spend the greatest number of waking hours, use most of my energies and give my thought, exercise my imagination, and use my creativity.

There are few "routine" decisions that I make. However, included in them are the approval of budgets, expenditures in excess of a given amount, the hiring of top executives, pricing, product approval, and the selection of advertising campaigns and programs.

One who aspires to apply the Christian teachings in business soon finds that many business decisions have a moral as well as an economic dimension. Almost all decisions which involve relationships between men invariably have a deep moral implication. Many decisions which appear on the surface to be primarily of an economic or technical character ultimately involve the well-being of men and, therefore, have moral implications as well. Thus, the choice of a product or plant location, the quality of raw supplies, prices paid or charged, etc., can and often do have a moral impact.

The quality and nature of one's moral concerns is, naturally, influenced by one's experience, background, and those aspects of the drama of life which have most profoundly etched themselves on one's soul and character. In this conjunction, I feel that a few details of my experience may be germane to the subject.

During the Second World War, I spent over a year in Europe in the occupied sections of Poland. Only for a brief time was I under the Germans; most of the time I was under Soviet occupation. Because of my great interest in history, I tried to evaluate the developing drama not only in terms of how it affected me personally, but what it meant as a human phenomenon. I was eager to discern from that myriad of grim, brutal, and seemingly irrational events and actions an underlying purpose. I came to the conclusion that, to the extent that religion is a search for a meaning of life, what unfolded in front of my eyes was a religious phenomenon, albeit without God. In broadest terms, it represented a quest for economic and social justice. I also realized that the dynamic power underlying man's contemporary dream for economic justice and equality of opportunity was captured and then manipulated by ruthless men for their own ends. Yet the urge itself, for economic and social justice, was authentic and genuine. I felt that the tragedy of our times lies in the fact that the church failed to identify herself with these powerful and justifiable aspirations of modern man. At the same time, I was convinced that the teachings of Jesus, which primarily pertain to how men must live together to enjoy a rewarding and fulfilling life, provide a sound, relevant, and rational basis for coming to grips with this drive of man. Upon returning to America, I concluded that business may be the most important medium for meeting man's contemporary aspirations for economic justice and equality of opportunity, and that businessmen, as individuals, may be the most influential agents for constructive change in building God's kingdom on this earth. Furthermore, it seemed to me that business and businessmen not only can be a channel for the implementation of economic justice and equality of opportunity, for which, indeed, most contemporary revolutions are being fought, but that they can help to bring this about without bloodshed, violence, or sacrifice of the ideals and institutions of the Christian world, that they can help it take place by the voluntary association of free men rather than the use of ever increasing coercive power of central government. Business—the production and distribution of goods and services—has become the central activity in our world today, and industrial might is the decisive factor in the way people and nations live, in the scope of their influence and in the dimensions of their power.

I have become convinced that the Christian businessman and manager must become the transforming agent in our society if our civilization is to survive and, more importantly, emerge victorious in the present struggle for human hearts, minds, and souls.

The development of modern productive processes indicates that the tendency toward further division of labor, higher specialization, and more intensive teamwork will continue to be the pattern of growth in business. This, in turn, will result in a more managed society and make the business manager an even greater factor of influence than he has been heretofore. Yet, whether this pattern of development will bring about a greater sense of fulfillment, a more meaningful life to modern man, and significant progress, or whether it will continue as a growth without a sense of real purpose is not an open and shut case. If the present trend prevails, then all that the so-called progress of business will mean is a further commercial exploitation of the pleasure motive, and further concentration of man's comfort, convenience, and leisure. This, if not checked, will bring an eventual deterioration. Which road will be chosen will depend primarily on what the leaders of our society and, I believe, specifically the Christian businessmen will be doing right now. It will depend on what image they will develop of themselves, pertaining to their function in our nation and our world.

Our society, economically and socially, has undergone a tremendous change in the last one hundred years—since the advent of the technological era. It has changed from a rural society, economically based on the labor of the family unit, to an industrial society. In the rural society the basic productive process was performed within the framework of a family husbandry. The modern productive process necessitates that we work in highly specialized and interdependent teams. The larger the team, the more complicated and interdependent it becomes.

Let me illustrate this. One hundred years ago most goods and services used by a man were produced by his own family unit or in the immediate vicinity of the community to which he belonged. But now, even a slice of bread, a carton of milk, have gone through literally hundreds of hands before they reach our tables. We wear clothes containing wool which may have been produced in Australia, cotton in Egypt, or silk in Japan. We probably carry a watch made in Switzerland, or other things which were produced or made of resources from any corner of the world. Economically in modern times men are forced to live together. However, spiritually they are lonely.

In the process of economic change many men have been uprooted. The concepts of togetherness developed against the climate of a different time do not pertain anymore and, unfortunately, no new contemporary concept has been developed.

The modern workshop is increasingly becoming a gathering place of people who live anonymous lives—anonymous in terms of not knowing one another or the purpose of their work. In most modern shops few people even know how their own labor contributes to the ultimate product in whose production they participate. Thus, a society is being created which is comprised of a lonely crowd socially uprooted, spiritually nonbelonging, and personally anonymous. This phenomenon is true both inside and outside the Iron Curtain, as I observed it at the time I was under Soviet occupation. I think future historians will name our age, "The Era of the Lonely Man." This loneliness of contemporary man may be one of the reasons why modern dictators have been able to rally men around themselves with such great speed and create committed followers. They seem to have understood the deep hunger of modern man to belong, to feel a community of destiny with other human beings.

Modern productive processes require men to work in teams. The nerve center of every team is the manager. Some business managers of large corporations influence and touch by their decisions thousands and sometimes hundreds of thousands, but even the humblest line manager influences to a great degree those entrusted to him. Thus, his responsibility and opportunity for Christian witness is profound.

How he will touch these lives, what influence he will exert will depend greatly on how he sees himself and how he views his position, his work, his responsibility, and the material and human resources at his command.

Does the manager who thinks of himself as a Christian have at the present time an image which encompasses his basic faith and its pertinence to his daily pursuits? I do not believe so. Quite the contrary, on the whole I feel that the average Christian businessman patterns his conduct and objectives by the existing rules of the economic game and, in fact, quite frequently acts and lives with a split personality —one reserved for Sundays and another for workaday pursuits. He may want to be a nice fellow, but this will not do; for, in order to be effective, he must first discern a conscious, cohesive, contemporary image of himself and his function and destiny. Now, within the framework of Christian teaching, there exists a fascinating concept that is pertinent to this image. This is the concept expressed in the parable of the talents that all of life is a relationship of trust. This simply means that whatever we have we have as trustees for the duration of our lives. It must be apparent even to the unbeliever that nothing—not a single hair—can we take with us when the span of our life has been completed. In a true sense the only freedom we have is that of being either good or bad trustees. All other choices in our lives are preconditioned by circumstance. The choice of our mate or home or job often is independent of our will and conscious intent. Yet the choice of doing right or wrong is always our own. Following Christ's example, we can always choose the cross. This is our free choice.

It is in conjunction with this concept of life being a relationship of trust that I feel the greatest development of Christian thought and practice is ahead of us, not behind us; that Christianity is the religion of the future more than of the past; that, as the Christian businessman embarks on a search for a more contemporary understanding of Christ's teachings as they pertain to modern society, he will receive insights which will lead him to the transformation of man and his surroundings. This, admittedly, will take revolutionary thinking. It may require a painful process of abandoning old comfortable concepts which have been built against a climate of a different civilization and necessitate the blazing of new trails. In an era that is enamored of science, I like to

110

think of Christ's teachings as the scientific rules of human conduct leading to fulfillment and growth.

The businessman who will view his function in this light as a trustee will be eager to develop the best know-how and skill to give him a chance to be successful. For he must be economically successful if he is to carry important witness.

I am sure he will have to take on faith that Christ's teachings are pertinent to every area of life; that they are as significant in our modern society as they were in the first century; that they are as true in Berlin or Moscow as they are in Washington or New York, and, finally, that they are as meaningful in business as they are in our personal life or church life.

I do not want to imply that successful business (as success is understood now by many businessmen) can be developed or conducted only in the framework of Christian concerns.

If success is equated with moneymaking alone, then there are undoubtedly some areas of business where men can be successful even by applying ruthless and immoral methods, but these are likely to diminish. At the moment it is almost impossible to build a lasting business institution on such premises, because most businesses which aspire to last must gain the confidence of those whom they serve in order to prosper. In the future, concern and ethical behavior toward employees will be as much a prerequisite of success in business as integrity in dealing with the public is now. It seems almost self-evident that where at one time technical know-how or the availability of capital was essential to business success, the building of an outstanding managerial team is the essential ingredient of success at this time, and experience has shown that economic incentive alone is not enough to attract the best people. If the qualities of truthfulness, integrity, concern for one's fellowman, and the ability and will to act in a fiduciary responsibility are identified with the Christian, then I submit that the Christian combines the ideal qualities of character and attitude which make an outstanding business manager. Businesses now and more so in the future will seek out these men, not only because they are "nice fellows," but because men with these characteristics will, from the standpoint of pure business considerations, be the best qualified to build outstanding and lasting institutions.

I am sure that the future Christian businessman, because of his general concerns, will try to move into a position of broad influence and to be in the mainstream of life where decisive battles are fought.

I am also convinced that the Christian businessman must take another look at the following four areas.

1. The first pertains to the manner in which men participate in the fruits of their labors. I feel that if we are to grow in a significant way, then a new concept based on incentive participation of those responsible for results will have to emerge. Presently most well-motivated employers think more in terms of giving than sharing. Yet giving, no matter how nobly motivated, will result in a system which will ultimately soften our muscle and bring boredom and stagnation. Sharing, on the contrary, means participating both in blessings and problems. It will stimulate a sense

of adventure and personal responsibility. Fortunately, in this country many companies have already embarked on profit sharing plans or stock sharing plans. To me, this is an indicator that businessmen with vision realize the importance of this approach.

2. The second pertains to the problem of employment. We must realize that unemployment is not wholly an economic problem. In fact, it is essentially a moral and psychological problem. Those who have been unemployed, who could not get a job, know the devastating impact of unemployment on the integrity of man, even on those men who can afford the economic rigors of unemployment. What affects man's integrity is the idea that he is not needed. I do not claim to have an answer to this problem, but I believe it is one which Christian businessmen must face with courage and a spirit of search.

3. We must take another look at the basic man in an industrial or commercial unit. We cannot continue to consider him as a hired hand only. He is not just a commodity. We must recognize that he is a human being and find ways to permit him to grow in depth, know-how, effectiveness, service, and self-respect.

4. We must find a way of removing the harmful anonymity of men in business. Man cannot be considered as a clock number. He is a member of a team, and his importance must be viewed in this light.

If we continue to seek single-mindedly, I am sure we can discern an ideology and develop a practice which will catch the imagination of the workingman around the world—

whether he be in the West, behind the Iron Curtain, or the heart of black Africa. We shall then turn the tide in the contemporary struggle for human minds and souls; for this is the uppermost concern of men around the world.

It is well to remember that the Communists have an image of how society ought to be ordained which is relevant to the problems of the modern industrial world, however vicious the results may be. We lack such an image, but there is no reason why we cannot develop a dynamic way of life which will show how obsolete is the Communist theory, how vicious is its practice, and, what is most important, how truly contemporary is the Christian view of life.

The main resources on which I depend are the Bible, devotional literature, prayer, and the quest for guidance. Contact with committed businessmen, particularly those in the Laymen's Movement, has given me much help in finding many answers, pointed to new directions, and provided a sense of reassurance and belonging, particularly at times when I find myself in "lonely places." Literature dealing with moral issues in society and business has been a great aid; but, on the whole, resources which have a direct, immediate, or contemporary relevance to the implementation of Christian ideals in business are, indeed, very few. There is a profusion of technical literature concerning management; but technical literature without the broader premises of man's purpose and function are not enough. Most of this literature is impersonal, and I am not sure that it is always a guarantee of constructive results in the long run.

Due to the increase of specialization in our society, few

ministers have a firsthand understanding of business, its rigors, and its problems. Most of those in the ministry have only a descriptive knowledge of business; rarely do they know the pressures, tensions, and responsibilities which businessmen face in practical circumstances. Thus, their answers are more often theoretical than relevant, and few businessmen seek the counsel and advice of the ministry concerning their professional pursuits. If the church is to be relevant to our lives, it must find ways for some of the clergy to gain an intimate knowledge of the business institution, which is now central to the lives of peoples and nations. What appears to me as being needed is an approach which would be scientifically sound yet morally oriented—a theology of work, a philosophy of business, a theory which would include business as one of the phenomena of total life, that would explain business activity not only as a means of making a living but as a way of leading a meaningful life.

My statement would be incomplete if I did not devote a few words to the actual attempts we have undertaken to implement some of the ideas expressed.

First, we have developed a profit-sharing plan which, in our industry, is somewhat unique. It is based on the premise that those who produce results must participate in these results. We stress to our people that we "give" them nothing —that we share what we produce together. We have been contributing no less than twenty percent of our profits yearly into our fund, and we continually take steps to review and improve our existing plan. The profit-sharing plan includes all employees, and we now have non-supervisory, non-managerial employees who have developed up to $15,000 of vested interest after a participation of eleven years in the plan. By the way, I should mention that we do not look at our profit-sharing plan as an immediate or direct incentive. Primarily, it creates a broad climate, a token of conviction that the company is committed to the concept of sharing. We make it clear that by sharing we mean sharing both the problems and the blessings. When problems have arisen, our people have shared in them with a spirit of stewardship and concern.

One of our most successful policies is what we call the "open door" policy, which means that any member of our company knows that he can have a hearing with anyone in the company, including the president, without fear of reprisal. In this we follow a procedure whereby an employee first meets with his immediate supervisor; if this proves unsatisfactory, the employee then has the opportunity to discuss his situation with the department head to whom his supervisor reports, and then, following channels of responsibility, has the opportunity to go to the president. I must state that our employees rarely ask to see me; I receive such requests not more than a few times each year, and almost always it is with good reason. This practice has been most beneficial. Because this is a stated policy of the company, our supervisors do not feel that things are done behind their backs. With the permission of those who request a hearing, it is often possible to bring to the supervisor a situation of which he would otherwise be unaware. The existence of this "right" also, undoubtedly, imposes discipline on those who might otherwise misuse their authority. I feel that this policy has been responsible for a general sense of freedom in the company. Yet it has never interfered with performance or commitment to objectives.

We have made counsel in the area of personal problems available to our people. These matters pertain to their family life, legal problems, financial situations, etc. When circumstances justify, we try to provide the help of a lawyer, physician, financial counselor, or whatever the situation may require. We feel that we have been able to be a factor of constructive influence in many serious situations. Our personnel manager has those qualities of character and concern to which people respond with confidence and trust. We have been unusually successful, particularly in the area of family relations and in questions concerning divorce. Because we make legal advice available when circumstances justify, we are often approached with requests for help when employees contemplate divorce. Our practice is to listen to their problem and then indicate that they are welcome to contact the company's lawyer for further advice, if they so desire. I daresay that not more than fifty percent of those who talk to us contact our attorney, and of those who do contact him, only an infinitesimal percentage ever enter into divorce proceedings. The company lawyer, by the way, never acts as counsel should the employee go on with the case. His function is limited to listening. Should he be requested, he will direct the employee to a competent and reputable attorney. Our experience in this area shows that what people in our industrial society need is an "ear" which will listen with concern and interest; a factory or workshop is a natural place in which such an "ear" can be provided.

As our company grew, it required the services of professional managers. It became evident that through an ordinary recruiting program it would be difficult to obtain the services of people who were both experienced and deeply committed to the application of religious values in business. Thus, if we were interested in having such men operate in our enterprise, we would have to develop them ourselves. We further came to the conclusion that if our objective was to build an institution which hopefully would set a pattern for other businessmen similarly motivated (and not be just another "successful" business), we would have to accomplish this goal with the help of men with both talent and commitment. Inasmuch as the commitment in these men had to be developed, we attempted to secure primarily the services of unusually bright young men, in most cases recent college graduates, who had the native talent and ability, and who were open to adventure, to growth, and to experiment. We were looking for men and women capable not only of becoming successful business people but of having the potential to become business statesmen.

As a result of these discussions, our young people's program was born. In the three years since this program got underway, we have hired approximately fifteen people. All but three of these people are still with us. Six of them came from Harvard Business School. Most of them were hired during the past two years. On the whole, our experience is most encouraging. It is reassuring to know, first of all, that young people are receptive to the idea of bringing a moral force into business; that they find a spirit of adventure in it; that so many of them ask that their business careers offer more than just a means of making a living; and that the idea of business being conducted on a high ethical plane seems to them not only possible but natural.

It is our conviction that most of those young men whom we hired have joined our company primarily because they felt there was real adventure in trying to build this kind of business. This ought to be reassuring to all businessmen who seek to apply Christian principles in their enterprises.

Furthermore, most of our young people are unusually industrious, are willing to work long hours, and are sensitive to the human and ethical values which we try to stress. Their presence in the company has been a constructive influence and imperceptibly has permeated our enterprise with the spirit of experimentation, with sensitivity to growth and openness to new systems, methods, and procedures. Some of the young people have made unusually effective contributions both to the growth of our business and to the development of a Christian business institution.

Most of the young people have done well in the company. One of them has become the head of all of manufacturing and is in charge of three plants with a force of approximately five hundred people. Another is the director of our marketing, with full responsibility for marketing policy and product development. Most of the others have also done well and, we believe, have accepted and discharged responsibility in a fraction of the time which would be considered customary in the normal business process. Three have left for good positions in other companies, helped on their way, we think, by their experience with us.

We feel that creativity adds to the total adventure of life and gives meaning to man's activity. We are committed to the development of an institution which places important value on the creative effort and the development of man on all levels of the company.

Within our organization, we have been able to discover people of promise and talent who have rapidly developed into outstanding members of the firm. We have designers who were once sewing machine operators; a production manager who was formerly a utility boy in our production unit; a personnel manager who was a secretary; a buyer who was a clerk; an assistant production manager who was a floor girl, and office and production supervisors who came from the ranks of the company—all this has transpired in just a five-year period.

As a result of our commitment to creativity, we have also been able to contribute importantly to new technology and art in the field in which we are engaged.

One of the most perplexing problems which faces managers who attempt to apply Christian principles in business is what to do with men who are incompetent. This problem becomes even more complex when the incompetent employee is a man of fine character and good purpose. The injunctions of Jesus would require an attitude of charity and understanding. Yet the first law of business is survival. On the surface this seems to be contradictory. A statement by the late

Moorehead Wright, a dedicated Christian and longtime executive of the General Telephone Company, "to be incompetent or to tolerate incompetence is immoral," sheds light on this issue, and we have found it most helpful. Except for disciplinary action, we have never dismissed an incompetent employee without providing him with sufficient time to find other employment. An employed person enjoys a bargaining position which permits him to find a new home and better pay than if he were unemployed. We have found that few of those who have left our company have ever taken unfair advantage of this policy. Most of them have been able to find a new responsibility which was better suited to their talents. The extra expense which this policy sometimes creates represents an infinitesimal part of the cost of doing business; yet it has been of immense help to many of our people.

Our recently established Committee on Justice also holds great promise. It consists of members of various departments and deals with questions of justice not only in relationships with our own people but in those external contacts with customers, suppliers, competitors, etc. We envision for this committee an ever increasing scope of interest and activity.

In conclusion, I feel I must answer the question which I am sure many of those who will read this statement will ask. "Have these policies worked?" If the injunction that "by your fruits you shall be known" is true, then they have, indeed, worked very well, for we have developed a company which seems able to resolve its problems through direct contact with its own people in a climate which appears to provide freedom, purpose, and opportunity for growth. We have grown each year since our inception in both profit and volume—with the exception of one year when we were ahead in profit but not volume, and this was due solely to supply shortages. Over a period of the last five years we have grown five to six times more rapidly than our industry. We are the recognized leader in innovation, and many of our designs have become standards for the industry as a whole. From an initial investment of $10 we have built a volume which will this year exceed $10,000,000 and place us in the upper one percent of the entire garment industry. We have been able to sustain this growth from profits and without any permanent outside financing. In the last few years we have been able to enter other fields of business endeavor with great success, despite the fact that our new activity is in a highly competitive area.

The attempt to implement Christian principles in business gave us a sounder basis from which to deal with economic problems, and in the ultimate analysis we are certain that this is the main reason for our success.

FARMING IS AN
EXCITING FRONTIER   *Richard C. Waybright*

What is my job and what does it mean to me? My job is farming. I was born on a farm in 1930 of parents whose ancestors for many generations had been farmers. Our farm was somewhat above the average in our general area. In those days children on the farms were expected to help with the chores. This began at the age of six or seven. Little by little I learned to accept responsibility for certain chores and received commendation when they were done well. But the economic depression and the drought that followed made agriculture rather unattractive as a life vocation. The long hours of hard work and the inconveniences of country living at that time were discouraging. In fact, there was a popular expression to the effect that if you couldn't do anything else, at least you could farm.

When I entered high school it was no longer taken for granted that the boys from the farms would become farmers. Each one of us was expected to make a definite choice of vocation. In spite of the dim prospect for the farmer I definitely chose agriculture. My chief motive was a deep feeling that the working and living conditions of the farmers could be and ought to be improved. This then became my challenge in life.

When I completed the courses at high school I had the option of going to an agricultural college but chose instead to go directly into the practical business of farming. I had become a member of the national organization called Future Farmers of America, and this group definitely encouraged practice rather than theory. There was much wisdom and encouragement from attending meetings, meetings of local chapters and of state organizations. Presently the Pennsylvania organization awarded me the Keystone Farmer Degree and sent me to the meeting of the national organization in Kansas City to receive the American Farmer Degree. This trip made an indelible impression on my outlook to the future. Observing methods of farming in the Middle West and having fellowship with men of humble origin who had become heads of industry and government greatly encouraged me to accept more responsibilities of leadership on the local scene of farming. I decided to increase my efforts to bring about some of the changes that farming so sorely needed. I always cherished the hope that our neighboring farmers would be moved to follow an example of better methods.

In all this my Christian convictions made their contribution. As my horizon expanded with reference to the needs and methods of farming, I felt a growing sense of responsibility to the Creator of the universe, the God who made this "good earth" and made man to till the soil. I took to heart the many references in the Bible to man's need for food and to God's abundant provision for that need. I noted also the several instances in which Jesus showed his concern for the hungry. Moreover, I began to feel that one of the major causes of conflict among tribes and nations, almost from the beginning of time, has been the lack of enough food or proper food and the thirst for survival. Only a small percentage of what is spent today on armaments would enable us to teach the hungry nations of the world to feed themselves properly without recourse to violence. I felt that much of the money that the church in its missionary work spends on hospitals, medical care, and other human welfare could better be spent on teaching the backward peoples of the earth to meet their own basic physical needs, especially the need for adequate food and proper diet. People then would also be more responsive to the gospel.

So I felt a special call to do everything possible in my small corner of the earth to set a modest example of helping to provide food for the world by helping to improve the facilities and methods of the food producers.

My lot as a farmer has been cast in a time of vast improvements in the technology of agriculture. This is both an explanation of and a comfort for the fact that so few people enter the profession of agriculture, less than three percent of our nation's population. More are not needed. In spite of the ruthless exploitation of fertile soil, the reduction of acreage through housing and industrial development, recreational parks, highway construction, and so forth, the large scale of modern farming and the technological improvements have brought it about that there is still enough food for everybody and, indeed, until recently a burdensome surplus of crops. Now if we only had more adequate methods of distribution there would not be a hungry mouth in America. Nevertheless, on the small farms that do most of the agriculture in Pennsylvania and Maryland, there is still great need for better methods and better facilities for working and living.

Accordingly we have pioneered in a number of agricultural practices that are new in this general area. Among these are milking parlors away from barn and feed odors, the six-bottom plow, the controlled heat drying system for hay, dry lot feeding, and automatic bunk feeding, diversion ditches to prevent soil erosion, the chisel plow instead of the moldboard plow to conserve moisture, mineral conservation and replacement to prevent depletion of the soil, artificial insemination to upgrade the herd, liquid manure handling system, the cement trench silo, the slatted floor and climate controlled barn, and a dairy processing plant on our own farm to provide our area with locally produced and processed quality dairy products. We have also studied the science of animal nutrition and have learned to release much more of the plant proteins for better human diets. As a result of these new methods, the dairy part of our farming has steadily enlarged, and during the past twenty-five years our farm herd of cows has grown from sixteen to 275. The farm with which we started about twenty years ago has expanded to include five farms with a total of 1023 acres. In addition we operate two farms with 215 acres on a "lease" basis.

In addition to these great changes in conserving the soil, improving the crops, and revolutionizing the milk industry in this area, we have introduced parallel changes both in sowing and in harvesting the crops. I assume that most of the labor-saving devices through mechanization and automation in farming during the past decade are known to the readers of these lines. Together they constitute a veritable revolution, so that it is possible for one man today, through improved ground tillage equipment and harvesting machinery, to produce the same number of pounds of beef and gallons of milk that ten men could produce twenty years ago.

This means much in terms of human value. Not only is there a large measure of satisfaction both to management and labor in the greater productiveness of the man-hour, but the work itself sheds all servile implications and takes on more sense of dignity. Our laborers are more content than they were under the old methods. The workday has been greatly shortened, and this release of time has enabled the farmer and his helpers to have higher standards of living, to reach higher levels of human satisfaction, better education for their children, and more participation in intellectual and even artistic activities. For more than ten years there has been no sign of dissatisfaction on the part of our employees. There is no forty-hour workweek, but the weekly take-home pay for our men is from $90 to $150. Moreover, the new developments in our work have released great numbers of workmen for other lines of employment. Modern methods and the new technology have brought it about that farmers no longer need to spend most of their time and energy in feeding themselves and their families.

I have always tried to be personally involved in the various operations of our farm and in the lives of those who help us in the work. I believe firmly in the great worth of the individual in the sight of God and have tried to cultivate in myself and my fellow workmen on the farm a sense of individual calling and responsibility. Because of the human elements involved in farming I am convinced that it would be a disaster to let American agriculture default completely to large corporations.

Because such a large percentage of young men and women today, capable and well-intentioned young people, go into other sciences, useful but less basic than agriculture, and because most of them have no opportunity to realize the necessities for farming and the possibilities for human satisfactions and human service in farming, we have been concerned to spread in every way this information about the new agriculture. Through farmer organizations and agriculture extension services we seek to stimulate interest among high school and college students in the arts of animal and soil husbandry, in the conservation of fertile soil areas, and in the vast possibilities of long-range human service through modern scientific agriculture. And there have been results.

Already some of our neighbors have adopted many of the methods they have seen in operation on our farm, and others have asked us, with our modern machinery and our more productive methods, to take over the cultivation of their animals and acres, thus releasing them to engage in lucrative service in town or city while still living in the ample comforts of the country.

The Pennsylvania Agricultural Service is taking measures to proclaim the merits of our new methods. In 1962 the Service presented our farm with the highest possible award, the Master Farmer Award. This has been helpful in spreading our gospel of human service through soil stewardship and animal husbandry.

There are three owners and managers of our farm, and we employ eleven other workers. We are concerned about them as individuals. We try to inculcate in them a sense of the dignity and worthwhileness of their jobs. To that end we maintain a pay scale that frees them from the mere hand-to-mouth existence which constitutes the plight of so many workers in private-enterprise farming. Our workers are provided with comfortable working conditions and powerful, efficient machinery that are calculated to remove all sense of drudgery from their jobs. Our helpers are not transients. They are guaranteed at least one increase in wages each year as they become more proficient in their particular jobs on the farm. They receive rewards for work especially well done. They are given opportunities to improve themselves, and as they develop their skills they receive more responsibilities and more freedom to make decisions of their own. Four of the young men who have been in our employ have gone on to further their education at agricultural and other colleges, and this we encourage. One of these men has begun studies for the Christian ministry.

These, I believe, are some of the "Christian dimensions" of my job.

WHERE ORGANIZATIONAL SYSTEMS MEET

Paul Wilbor

The Task

I am a career government employee with some twenty-five years of service in the Federal Government. I am employed by the Aeronautical Systems Division of the Systems Command of the United States Air Force, located at Wright-Patterson Air Force Base, Dayton, Ohio. Our business is the development and procurement of the aerospace military systems for the maintenance of superior power for the national defense. We, together with the aerospace industries, develop and produce the aircraft, missiles, components, and supporting ground equipment for America's strategic, defensive, and tactical forces throughout the world. To do this job we have about nine thousand people in the Division, consisting of some fourteen hundred Air Force officers and seventy-six hundred career civilians. The annual budget for contracting with industry, research institutions, and universities is approximately six and one half billion dollars. The Division deals with two to three thousand industrial contractors each year and with about three hundred universities and research institutions. We maintain field offices at all the test centers and other development agencies in the continental United States, and with the NATO countries through a European office. This should give you some idea of the magnitude of the operation in which I participate. It is, if you will, a large bureaucracy.

But it is not the size of my organization that is most relevant to the subject at hand. Rather, it is the behavior of the organization and the responses it must make to the total environment in which it exists. The internal environment of structure, organization, hierarchy, and operations really becomes significant only if seen in the perspective of the external factors that so strongly affect our orientation and motivation. Being at the center of the military struggle with the Soviets, we must be responsive to what they are doing technologically in both offensive and defensive weapons. We must compare this to our knowledge of our own national technological efforts and arrive at programs and systems which will maintain the balance-of-weapons superiority. This task calls for a continuing and deep relationship with the scientific community of the nation not only for their appraisals of our proposals but also for launching new research efforts.

Since industry is the source of all our military hardware, we must work with companies to assure they are capable of translating new ideas and knowledge into effective systems and equipment. Since the taxpayer's dollar is the means of getting this done, the where and how of the dollars getting spent pulls into play political and economic factors at the national and the local levels. All this must be done in a framework of constraints such as dollar limitations of the budget; the full play of a free enterprise system of business; maximum competition; preferential treatment for small business; flowing of hardware work into areas of economic distress or dislocation; and with all higher levels of government, both executive and legislative, reviewing and second-guessing each major decision.

Overriding this structure of complex relationships, there is, of course, the security problem and Department of Defense policy which constrains the content of what may be said and to whom. I am not trying to impress you with the toughness of the work but to indicate the multiplicity of interests to which we must be responsive, and to identify the many sources of the single constant in the environment—which is *change*.

With an exploding technology interacting with all the other interests I have described, we must be readily responsive to change—change in weapons; change in their performance; change in the numbers of them we buy; change in the rates of their production; change in costs; change in the methods of testing the weapons; change in the methods for contracting for them; and change in the manner in which we manage them. Over against this constancy of change there is the other background factor—the urgency and critical importance of *time*. We are in competition with the military efforts of the Communist world. There is nothing leisurely or casual in our tasks.

Organizational Structure

There is one more thing that bears on the kinds of decisions I must make in my work. It has to do with the peculiar structure which results from the combining of military personnel with civil service personnel. Each of these career systems has its separate, specialized scale of values and procedures covering incentives, promotions, recognition, compensations, transfer, mobility, and codes of conduct.

Basically the military system is built around the idea of the development and interchangeability of its officers, while the Civil Service system is oriented to the idea of occupational specialization and to the concept of equal pay for equal work. This mixing of differently oriented personnel into a single structure produces relationships and a way of operating not found in a purely civil government agency, in a purely military organization, or in a private concern. Whereas the conventional unmixed organization has a two-dimensional power structure, that is, the formal organization and the informal organization, the military-technical organization is in six dimensions: the formal integrated organization, the informal integrated structure, plus a formal and informal structure for each of the military and the civilian components. This discussion of structures is pertinent to the behavior of all our people, including me, and consequently to the behavior of the entire institution.

My Job

So much for the environmental background—now to my job itself. I am one of three coordinate heads of the centralized management staff of the Division. One of my associates, an Air Force colonel, is the formal head of the organization. The other is a career civilian like me who specializes in the research and development processes. My specific area of concern is with the acquisition processes in all their aspects, between the Air Force and industry. Our staff consists of some one hundred and ninety senior specialists of all kinds: scientists, engineers, procurement specialists, production experts, and management analysts.

My work as an executive consists in laying out the objectives, guidance, timing, and resources allocations to our staff and, through them, to the rest of the organization. I am personally responsible for seeing that the required technical competence and effectiveness are built into all our undertakings and that we present credible and acceptable results to the upper echelons of the Air Force.

One further comment: As you have concluded by now—if you haven't become lost in all this bureaucratic terminology

135

—my work and responsibilities lie wholly in the field of management. Now there are probably a million definitions of management, but basic to all of them is the concept that management essentially consists of getting things done through people. Such things as organization, policies, control, personnel systems, formal hierarchies, and the like are really only the tools of management to get people to do the things that management has determined to be necessary or desirable. Herein lies the challenging dichotomy of all management, whether we are talking about top, middle, or lower management, or whether we are considering private versus public management. The basic and ever present question or problem is, when and how much to use the power and authority of formal rank, position, and hierarchical prestige instead of the human considerations of understanding, empathy, motivation, and respect for the dignity and interests of the individual. It is in this area of interpersonal and intergroup relationships that perhaps some of the answers we are seeking may be found. I will therefore attempt to center my discussion around these relationships.

Let us look at some cases. In working with industry my division has a continuing relationship with each military contractor that covers the life cycle of a military idea from the discovery of new knowledge to the final delivery of the last piece of hardware. Time is measured in years. We live with these people and with all their problems through the planning, financing, contracting, and performance of their efforts. This quite naturally leads to a great deal of subjective and objective evaluation and appraisal of the strengths and weaknesses of many companies and of their key personnel. This result is built into the long and intensive relationship which is a cornerstone of the teamwork that must be carried out by industry and the government. What kinds of problems does this series of value judgments present to me as I make my personal decisions? Let us look at some specifics.

Profits

Several years ago the defense industry was making an effort to increase the profit margins the government allows in its contracts, and a top executive of one company was discussing the problem with a Congressional committee. One of the arguments he pressed most strongly was that, since the government would not allow his company to sell his products competitively to other governments, such as the Russians, it should compensate for this prescribed limitation by allowing his company wider profit margins. The reaction to this testimony of course came back to my agency which places hundreds of millions of dollars with the company each year.

The government dollar has provided the sustenance and growth of this company over the years. The company has extremely high weapons capabilities and know-how. Its resources and products are of vital importance to our military strength. Moreover, we in the government know and accept the absolute necessity of maintaining a healthy and profitable industry.

How should one react, in a personal sense, to this sort

of situation? You must keep in mind that, as an individual, you are meeting regularly with representatives of this company, participating in the decisions to put additional work in its plants, developing the criteria by which its proposals will be evaluated, and arranging for the analysis and evaluation of the costs and profits it is asking for in its new contracts and programs. Do you discount the executive's statement as one of shrewd political leverage and forget about it? Do you let it affect your judgment of the company affairs? Do you attempt to gauge the effect of such a statement on your associates and their judgments as you see them being applied? Would you openly discuss the statement with other officials of the company? Would you invest any concern in wondering whether the company really would sell its military products to the Communists, or try to, if there were no government constraints?

Let us look at another example in government-industry relationships. Because of my experience and participation in undertaking military programs with industry and in following through and getting them accepted by the higher levels of government, I have been able to be of help to several important companies. Some of these, at various times, have offered me employment at a much higher salary than the government affords. These offers have been made honestly and sincerely in connection with wanting my services and have had no ulterior motives.

I have consistently refused them for a number of reasons which are valid to me. But these offers always leave an unresolved component of judgment which overhangs my continued relationship with the companies. Can I be sure that my attitude toward these companies is not just a little more cooperative and perhaps prejudiced than it is toward equally good companies which have not approached me? Am I perhaps tempted to give them advance, inside information or to act a little more quickly in getting answers they need from the government? How do I adjust myself to ensure that the relationship remains within normal boundaries?

Personnel

Now I would like to discuss some of my decisions that are much closer to my everyday life in the office and to the job of getting things done within the government. Quite aside from the matter of qualitative technical judgment, there arises in day-to-day interpersonal relationships the whole range of human considerations surrounding the motivation, enthusiasm, and effectiveness of the individual or group. What you did or said yesterday or did not do or say carries over into today's relationship. Today's interchange or action will accrue positively or negatively to the sum of the relationship and will affect dealings in the future. I have long since learned that, if I am concerned about developing the full potential of the people with whom I work, they must be given as much autonomy as possible in thinking and reaching decisions.

Now in most situations where I am trying to get people to do a job or solve a problem, I generally know—because of my longer and richer work experience—the type and character of the problem's solution or, if not that, the most useful approach which will yield a solution. One's first inclination, particularly if pressed for time, is to tell people what you think the solution is or should be, and to reinforce that judgment with the power and authority of your position. Unfortunately this mode of operation is found entirely too often in managerial situations.

If, however, you are genuinely and sincerely interested in people as people, and accept them as the most important and precious resource there is, your working with them will take on an entirely different character. You will take the time, invest the patience, and exercise the humility necessary to let these people discuss the why, what, how, and who of the problem or assignment as they feel it and think it. You will limit your role to penetrating questions, observations, and comments, all of which are designed to steer the ultimate course of action in the general direction in which you think it should go. Needless to say, this approach leads to considerable attrition in your own ideas and judgments. You never get exactly what you want, but you have made tremendous gains in the transfer of some learning on both sides, and you have created a far healthier attitude and willingness to get the work done. People will follow the agreed-upon solution because it is in large part theirs.

Some might label this type of leadership manipulative. It does have some of those characteristics. But it is manipulation in the direction of the kind of development and growth through which people become more valuable and effective to themselves, to the organization, and, in our case, to furthering some vital national objectives.

Morale

Earlier, I made quite a point about the frequency and velocity of change in our work, programs, and military equipment. This can present quite a problem in its corrosive effect on the attitudes, motivations, and effectiveness of our personnel. A good illustration can be found in the B-70 supersonic aircraft program about which so much controversy has appeared in the press.

The Air Force has supported the development of this manned aircraft and has argued that the present B-52 fleet should be replaced by a generation of superior manned weapons which will augment and strengthen the striking power of missiles. Our people agree with this viewpoint and further judge that the engineering, development, manufacturing, and testing problems are within the military arts and capabilities of the scientific, industrial, and government communities.

We started this program in 1955 with an initial estimate that the bird would be flying in 1959. We don't have the B-70 today, and it probably will be almost a year before it flies. Moreover, it will be only an experimental aircraft shell with no essential military firepower, bombing, or reconnaissance systems in it. Throughout the twisting, turning, changing history of this effort we have had to maintain an organization of good, dedicated people which, many times over, has gone through cycles of expansion and contraction.

There is a tremendous amount of challenging, creative technical and managerial work to be done in this program. How do you keep the people working on it from going sour and crossing the fatal line of cynicism and defeat? A couple of months ago, for example, within a span of some thrity days, the people in charge of this program had to make some twenty-five briefings to different government and industry groups, all with a different emphasis and content but all essentially in justification, defense, or promotion of the program. This kind of experience can be and is heavily fraught with psychic and intellectual impact on those involved. Despite the doubt, discouragement, and disappointment of the experiences, someone in my position dare not, as a designated leader, drop his level of confidence, or dilute his determination, or minimize his responses to new challenges. It would be so much more comfortable and easy to play the bureaucratic game of passing the buck for decisions, rolling with the punches, or placing the responsibility elsewhere. But this is not the way progress is made.

A Problem of Rank

I spoke earlier about the intermixture of military and civilian personnel adding additional dimensions to our organizational problems. Let us take up only a couple of facets.

142

As in the other examples cited, I approach this also from the standpoint of interpersonal relationships and the pertinent questions they raise.

My present military chief is a full colonel with some twenty years in the Air Force. His present job is the first exposure he has had to the technical industrial side of the Air Force. Most of his previous experience has been with flying and training operations. He has high capabilities in dealing with people, but he has the problem of gaining an incisive understanding of the technical environment in which he now finds himself. He will probably be in this job for three or four years, at the end of which time he will have gained a real knowledge and understanding of the total implication of his decisions. He probably will never come back to this same job.

Now the problem here is how much do you concern yourself with this man as an individual, not in the sense of his being boss or chief (you can live with almost anyone administratively) but rather of transposing yourself into his position and deciding how much does he (or do I) really need to know to make sound decisions? How do you provide this learning? At what rate can it be absorbed? When do you in critically significant cases take the decision away from him? You have several options of attitude and effort in these situations, but you finally have to strip off all the external considerations of rank, position, and career differences and deal with the relationship in purely human terms.

A Question

In drawing these examples from my work, I have tried in part to answer the first question put to me: *How do I see my job in terms of its value as a job and the personal stresses and pressures experienced within it?* Let me recapitulate briefly. I see my job as an important one through which I can make some sort of contributions, hopefully significant toward the achievement of national goals that, for the present, are vital to our survival. The job provides me with an opportunity to work with a large group of people who are similarly dedicated and motivated. It represents a challenge to every shred and particle of the endowments of intellect and talent which the good Lord has placed in my stewardship. As to pressures and stresses, they are tremendous and continuous, measured in any terms you might choose—time, effort, resourcefulness, impact on family life social calendar, self-confidence, and a constant adjustment to my personal scale of values.

When I reflect on the fact that the dollars and resources allocated to any one of our major programs would build and staff dozens of modern hospitals, considerably more schools, tremendous numbers of recreational or public utility facilities, I become acutely aware of the exorbitant price man has to pay for his inability to live with himself and his neighbor. On the other hand, I am keenly aware of what could happen to this nation and the entire community of the free world if we do not have the military shield or umbrella under which some ultimate peaceful solution to our international problem must come. By this yardstick, then, what are essentially wasteful expenditures are by definition mandatory. I am concerned with my job, I am responsive to what I see its demands are, and I like it.

A Tougher Question

The next question is tougher: *What are the Christian dimensions of the decisions and problems that I have to meet?* I see these dimensions at two clearly distinct levels or through two different perspectives. The first I will term the institutional or, perhaps better, the ideological level. If we start with the belief that the basic concepts of individual freedom, personal worth, and dignity all derive from God's love of mankind (which as Christians we see manifested in Christ), then the institutions which free men have built—whether economic, political, commercial, or spiritual—all reflect or embody that belief in varying degrees. Don't misunderstand me. I am not trying to mix apples and oranges, merely stating that some of the Christian values surrounding the individual are present in varying degrees in all free institutions. Now it is these same free institutions that are under attack by the Communist totalitarians, and these individual freedoms and values are implicit and integral to the institutions.

Therefore, as I see it, there are some vital issues at stake in this clash of ideologies, issues of grave concern to all Christians. It might well be pointed out that our free institutions are not without weaknesses and faults in the context of this strenuous struggle. It is not beyond reasonable limits of feasibility that the cold war is God's way of testing what his believers have done and will do institutionally with the freedoms and values he had made possible for us to enjoy. We need not, indeed we dare not, vitiate or destroy these institutions but rather must find some way to influence their scale of values so that they may become more effective in this contest for survival. With reference to the institution of free enterprise, I would raise the question, for example, as to why many modern corporations which now recognize and accept separate and distinct responsibilities to stockholders, management, public, employees, and labor cannot also accept responsible concern for the total national long-range welfare and existence. I cannot go along with Charlie Wilson's famous statement, while he was Secretary of Defense, that "what is good for General Motors is good for the nation." There is still a significantly wide base of opinion of this sort in corporations of major importance to our defense effort.

I would raise a series of questions along the same lines with respect to the institutions of government. For example, the decision-making processes for weapons are getting longer and more complicated each year. Every level in the executive and legislative branches must get in on the act, and each is assuming a larger role of expertise.

In some major weapon decisions, it now actually takes longer to get a final and durable government decision than it takes to do the technical and engineering work to develop the system. Many of these government people have not done their homework fully in reaching understanding, so that decisions are being made under extremely high conditions of uncertainty. Because of the very high rate of change growing out of our advancing technology, what they heard and understood last year does not apply to what they are getting this year in the military weapons program.

From another viewpoint, we need checks and balances in our form of democracy. But we certainly do not need to apply those checks and balances with archaic tools and techniques such as procurement laws and constraints that go back in history as far as the Civil War. Nor do we help ourselves by using budget and program justifications essentially in the same format cycle and detail used when the total Federal outlays were on the order of two to three billions per year. Remember that far back?

All that I am attempting to say is that there is tremendous need for improvement in our free institutions in this struggle for survival. Fortunately there is a small but growing awareness of these self-imposed limitations, but it is going to take time to remove them, and the key question is, do we have that much time?

There certainly are some Christian dimensions buried in all this. I think they have to do with such things as faith and confidence in one another, unshakable belief that, at least in part, what we are doing is God's will, and that we each have a very heavy responsibility to perpetuate and extend our Christian heritage. Is it just possible that, through expansion of the faith, we are entering a historical regime wherein we finally may have the opportunity to defeat the old cynical apothegm that "God is always on the side of the big army"?

Relationships

The second level or perspective of the Christian dimensions of my work lies in the interpersonal relationships I encounter in carrying out my job. Here the emphasis bears heavily on the commandment "love thy neighbor as thyself." The observance and practice of this commandment has been achieved but once in the entire history of the world. All we can do is to make a sincere, relentless, and unremitting effort to try. These efforts pull into play the positive Christian virtues of caring, humility, sharing, charity, suspension of final judgments, and reconciliation. Constantly working against these are the sinful characteristics and actions of selfishness, pride, exploitation of brother, and coldness. The fabric of every administrative and managerial situation is woven with the warp and woof of these factors. They are not explicitly discussed, but every action and reaction reflects them.

The workaday vocabulary for the positive virtues are usually such terms as helpful, understanding, cooperative, easy to deal with, unaffected, honest, objective—a good guy or a good boss. The negatives are the eager beaver, out-for-number-one, you can't trust that guy, be careful what you say to him, he has no respect for people, he has to hog the show, be in on every act. Some even use stronger, far less polite terms.

The practice of these virtues and the curbing of the vices, I am convinced, lies at the very heart of creative, imaginative, and progressive management. It is the only way, in my judgment, that you can create an environment of growth and enthusiasm contributing to the development of people. In large organizations such as mine, I would estimate that we actually realize or obtain less than half of our people's creative potential. Why? Because we set up blockages and inhibitions through using rank, power, and authority to control their behavior, not Christ's simple summary of the law.

The Final Question

You will recall that the final question had to do with *the resources available to me in forming my decisions and for supporting me as a person.* I share the common problem of all administrators in having to be informed of what is currently going on in my working environment. I do this by a considerable amount of reading of technical journals and of collateral literature. This reading is reinforced by attending many technical conferences of an informational type and by fairly regular travel to industrial plants and to other government agencies. This fairly well takes care of the technical input I need beyond that gained on the job itself. It is a fairly standard pattern in maintaining one's professional currency and competence.

My social activities provide little direct contribution to my decision-making problems. They serve the normal purposes of the personality demands for variety and relaxation in our human relationships.

As to the resources for the spiritual and motivational values we have been trying to develop, the cornerstone, of course, is faith and belief. Through prayer, meditation, and the sacraments, you offer to God a full review of the actions and decisions you have made and your evaluation of their fitness or appropriateness to your current level of understanding of his purposes and concern for you. When you have taken, or not taken, action which has led to alienating or transgressing against other people, you ask for forgiveness and accept the implicit responsibility to be equally forgiving of other people's transgressions. You don't invariably establish good contact, and in my case I believe this to be a corollary of the depth and scope of the concern, openness, and completeness with which I offer up my work to God. When it does come, the contact is like a freshening wind that carries away with it the trash and remnants of human weakness and at the same time brightens and burnishes the fixed values of the Christian landscape.

I don't find much in the current Christian literature that has direct and transferable value to my specific situation. There is a great deal of interchange needed across the religious and secular compartments of our lives. Christians need help in relating their faith to the problems they encounter at work, and I hope that the church's search for new ways to help them may be urgently and successfully pursued. Meanwhile, if this account of my own attempts to relate work and faith has helped, I am grateful.

SCRUBBING FLOORS IS
HARD WORK

Nadine A. Oyler
(as told to the editor)

I *have* to do cleaning and scrubbing. It's been the only way I can make money to finish raising five kids since my husband's death ten years ago.

It's hard work too. I don't believe for a minute that a mop can do the job in scrubbing kitchen and bathroom floors. Mops just redistribute the dust. I'm not afraid to get down on my knees and go at it. That seems to be unusual today and I could do two weeks of work every week, for all the women who want my help.

I get some satisfaction out of it too. Not that I would choose this kind of work if I had the education for some other jobs. But my mother was blind the last eleven years of her life and I had to stop school after one year in high school. Don't believe I didn't cry that fall when my friends went back for their sophomore year.

The good part of my work is that I am often with people I like. To some extent I can choose now which homes I'll clean, really which women I want to work for. I like to be sociable and enjoy the talk and friendliness of some homes and housewives. Not that I just stand around and gab.

And, when you ask me, I can agree that I like to go into a dirty house and make it clean. There's a satisfaction in doing a thorough job of cleaning a floor, a room, a whole house. Week by week I come to feel that this home is my responsibility and that this woman and family need my help. After a while I don't mind either if my job gets held up because of baby sitting (or pet care), telephone answering, bed making, and things like that. And I feel like part of the family at the lunch table.

I guess an important part of it is that people come to trust me. Maybe at 9 A.M. the wife explains that she must take the children shopping in Baltimore, and at noon her husband rushes in and out on his way to the golf course, leaving me taxi money. All day I work hard so that she'll be pleased with the clean house when she gets back. And I figure I work harder than usual (even though I get paid by the hour) to prove something to myself.

Why do I do that? I suppose you're right that I want

to think I'm a person people can trust. Or you could say that I just think people should be that way.

Do I relate these work attitudes to my Christian faith and my church attitudes? The answer is no. I never have thought things through like that. I've been attending Sunday school or church since I was a little girl, belonging to Lutheran churches since I was eight. I can't say I attend real faithfully, but I'm an active member of our Sunday school class and I believe the things that are taught there. Sure, I can agree, after you point it out, that my desire to be good at scrubbing and cleaning and to be trusted in my work probably has a lot to do with my belief in God and his creation and the purposes that God has for human beings. I just never thought much about it in that way.

BUILDING GOOD WILL
FOR RAILROADS   *George M. Crowson*

I have been invited to give an account of my convictions
and experiences as a Christian layman in the course of the
daily work at which I earn my living. Frankly, I am not
aware that either my convictions or my experiences along
the line of this invitation are more noteworthy than those
of any number of the people with whom I have had the
great good fortune to be associated in the course of my
working life. However, I do undertake to put my faith into
my work, and if my convictions and experiences can be of

155

value to others, I am glad to attempt this response to the challenge.

For some years after completing my schooling I was employed as a newspaper reporter in my native Missouri. Then in 1920 I was given the opportunity to join the Illinois Central Railroad at its headquarters in Chicago to assist in setting up what became one of the pioneer public relations programs in the railroad industry. Five years later, in 1925, following the death of my superior, I was given the immediate responsibility for the conduct of our public relations program. As these lines are written, in 1966, I have recently retired, after more than forty-five years in the public relations work of the "Main Line of Mid-America." Since my retirement from the Illinois Central I am offering my services as a counselor or consultant on matters of public relations and associated concerns of business management.

In the course of my working life in railroad public relations I have of course been involved in association with other railroad personnel and other public relations people. I have been a member of the Advisory Committee on Public Relations of the Association of American Railroads from its founding in the 1930's. I was one of the organizers of the Railroad Public Relations Association and served as its president in 1957-58. I am also a charter member of the Public Relations Society of America and was privileged to serve as its president in 1955. And I have been involved in the public relations activities of numerous civic and related organizations, including the Young Men's Christian Association of Metropolitan Chicago, the Chicago Chapter of the

American Red Cross, and the United Charities of Chicago. Also I have served the churches with which I have been affiliated during my life in the Chicago area in various capacities, including a certain amount of effort on their communications, both external and internal, which are an essential part of their public relations. Altogether it has been a rich and challenging experience, for which I am deeply and eternally grateful. This then is the background against which I must relate my convictions and experiences as a Christian layman in the course of my working life.

If I am to deal at all understandably with my convictions and experiences as a religiously motivated layman in the course of my daily work over these years, I believe I need to start with some exposition of my philosophy—my thinking —about the nature and content of public relations work—in plain words, what I conceive public relations work to be all about. I am all too painfully aware of the false notions that too many people seem to have about the nature and content of public relations work. Unfortunately it seems to be the misconception of entirely too many people that work in public relations consists for the most part in seeking public attention and/or public acceptance of the cause or client regardless of merit. It would seem to me that no religiously motivated layman could accept any such view of the field in which to earn his living. My own view of public relations—of what is involved in public relations work—is that it has to do with the conduct of the affairs of the enterprise being served in such a manner as to merit, to deserve, to win the knowledge, understanding, and support of the various groups of people who are related to the enterprise in one or more of various ways—as owners, as employees, as suppliers, as legislators, as regulators, as customers (of course), and, perhaps most importantly of all, simply as its friends and neighbors. That is the challenge of public relations to which our efforts were increasingly devoted during my years of employment by the Illinois Central Railroad, and it is the concept of public relations which I have endeavored to foster and to implement in the other circles in which I have been involved.

Of course I am well aware that every worthwhile occupation affords an opportunity to put religion to work—to make the way of life that Christ taught and exemplified come alive and have meaning these two thousand years later. I believe this is particularly true in the practice of public relations. To be effective in public relations, the practitioner must have and show the consideration for others which, it seems to me, is of the very essence of the Christian religion.

In the course of my work in public relations I have naturally done a considerable amount of writing, for writing is in its very nature one of the tools of the trade—the writing of addresses, of public statements, of answers to inquiries, of correspondence, of news and supporting material, and of any number of other things for conveying information and opinion by the written word. Speaking is another obvious means of communication with which the public relations worker must have more or less to do, and I have had the privilege of speaking on railroad and public relations subjects to a considerable number of audiences. But most of all,

I believe it needs to be said, public relations work consists of planning, of consultations, of research into basic materials and human motivation, of endless sessions with associates, with subordinates and with superiors, seeking always to find a better, a more acceptable, a more rewarding way of doing the various things that need to be done in the course of the enterprise. And that, let me emphasize, is public relations in action, in whatever undertaking it is involved.

With such a concept of public relations, opportunities are unlimited to exercise one's convictions and to amass one's experiences as a Christian layman. Indeed, I would be at some loss to undertake a public relations program for any employer or client except as an individual who accepts and strives to practice the code of conduct of a Christian layman.

I do not pretend that this has been my full-blown philosophy throughout my working life. I grew up in a Christian home, and I have been surrounded by Christian influences all my life. It is from such a background that I have found the resources for working out the concepts of public relations which I have developed over my years in the field. But I want to emphasize that my philosophy of public relations has been an evolution, a growth, drawing its concepts from the countless associations of a rich and rewarding working life.

Coming from a newspaper background where I had occasion to seek information from so many people in the course of my rounds, I was quite conscious at the beginning of my railroad experience that a great many, if not most, railroad people, officers as well as employees, were rather reluctant to talk about railroading outside their own immediate circles. As I thought about it I came to the conclusion that this was not because they were uninformed so much as that they did not believe it was the proper, the acceptable thing for them to do. An informed and articulate organization is a must in public relations, and this is particularly true in the case of a railroad or the railroad industry. There are few people anywhere who do not have some acquaintance with someone who works for a railroad, and their opinions of individual railroads and of the industry are bound to reflect what they see and hear among the railroad people of their acquaintance. Therefore I set out to do something about it on my own railroad. We began the publication and distribution to the key people in our organization of a monthly statement called "Things to Talk About," and these statements came to be reproduced in our company magazine, which goes to all employees of the railroad as well as to a considerable number of friends and neighbors. The very fact of providing "Things to Talk About" made it plain that we wanted our people to talk about railroading in the various circles in which they were involved. Results could be seen immediately, and they have increased over the years. I venture to say that there are no more articulate people in all business and industry than the people of the American railroads!

I believe it is essentially Christian to help people to become better informed and more articulate about the business in which they are engaged—not only because it contributes to the enterprise, but also and just as importantly because it gives them a greater sense of mission and adds to their reason for being.

Another place where public relations comes into play is in the handling of complaints. As I have encountered people who are antagonistic to railroads and have undertaken to find out why, I have discovered that almost invariably their antagonism stems from some complaint that has not been satisfactorily disposed of. On the other hand, I have also discovered over and over again that people who think well of railroads have had some memorable exposure to a railroad, or have had an unfavorable experience well offset by the way their complaint was handled.

One of the phenomena of railroading is that what makes for good or ill for one railroad is reflected in the case of every other railroad. I have often encountered people who have a grievance toward my railroad as a result of an unfortunate experience on another line, and, conversely, I have discovered that some of our best friends reflect favorable experiences with us elsewhere. All railroads run on the same public relations track.

That is why our public relations program for the Illinois Central Railroad was not directed toward winning friends and influencing people for our railroad alone but was equally devoted to increasing knowledge, understanding, and support for all railroads, our competitors as well as our connections. This has been reflected in our institutional advertising. At the time I came to the railroad, we embarked upon a program of regular advertising in all newspapers, weeklies as well as dailies, along our railroad, in the fourteen states in which the Illinois Central operates. This advertising has been continued without interruption and is recognized in advertising circles as a model program of public relations advertising. Never in the more than forty-five years of communicating in this channel with our friends and neighbors up and down the length of our railroad has anything been said that fails to reflect to the good of all railroads. And I believe this is an example of Christian conviction in action.

In dealing with complaints, all too often there is a real temptation to ignore some, particularly those which seem to have little merit. It has not been my decision alone, but the decision is one that reflects my own thinking and on which I have been a consultant, to treat every complaint and every complainant as we would have someone treat a complaint of ours—in other words, to apply the principles of the Golden Rule. Every complainant receives an acknowledgment of the complaint, and where it calls for corrective action, that action is taken. More often than not a representative of the railroad is requested to call on the complainant for a full, complete discussion of the matter. These calls are not made by professional complaint handlers, but by our people in the area who are familiar with all the circumstances and who often were involved in the incident out of which the complaint arose. Someone may question whether this is Christian conviction in action—I suggest that it is.

The same can be said about the handling of compliments. I believe it is good public relations to be just as meticulous in dealing with the good things that are said about us. That is why during all my years in the handling of our public relations program we never failed to acknowledge with appreciation and thanks a newspaper article or editorial that was complimentary to our railroad or that supported a position that meant something to us. And that was equally true of our correspondents who were complimentary to us or who reported pleasing incidents. Every one received a cordial "thank you." Again I would contend that this is Christian conviction in action.

One of the great misconceptions that many railroads have had to contend with is that the land grants that were made at the beginning of the railroad era to aid the pioneer railroads in opening up the country and leading to settlement and development are equivalent to the modern aids so lavishly given by the government for the support of transportation by water, road, and air. The difference is not readily apparent to a great many people, and indeed many textbooks have supported the belief that railroads are the beneficiaries of the early-day land grants. Not only did these grants make it possible for railroads to be built where there was no supporting traffic at the time, but the grants were made in alternate sections of the public land and prices were doubled on the remaining sections so that no outlay was involved.

How to deal with this misconception has been a continuing public relations problem for the railroads, especially for such as the one with which I spent so many years, which was aided in its construction by one of the original land grants. It has required patience and respect for the opinions of

163

others, and I believe real progress has been made in combatting what has often seemed one of the most trying barriers to the understanding and support that are our continuing goals in railroad public relations.

I mentioned earlier our public relations advertising. I should like to tell especially about one series of advertisements that we had some years ago, because I believe it has particular public relations significance, and I also believe it illustrates Christian concern and action. This series was based upon the idea that the distinguishing characteristic of a railroad is not in its equipment, its schedules, its rates—these are much the same among railroads—but in what is done over and above the bare bones of operation for the individual customer. In preparation for the advertising we made a survey of our entire organization, operating as well as sales and service personnel, to turn up cases where we had gone far beyond what we were called upon to do to personalize or to supplement our service. Out of a collection of hundreds of such incidents we selected a dozen, one for each advertisement in the series: the special handling of a carload of coal for a hospital that had run out of fuel; an advance payment of taxes, before they were due, to keep a school from having to close for want of funds; the personal efforts of a small-town station agent to locate and deliver to its owner a piece of baggage that had gone astray. They were really things that are done any number of times on any number of railroads near and far, but did they ever attract attention and get talked about! Though the series ran a good many years ago, our friends and neighbors up and down the railroad still talk about some of the stories we told.

Another development on the railroad for which I had the immediate responsibility was our good-housekeeping program. It was born in the depression of the thirties, when we were bending every effort to control expenses to avoid the bankruptcies that had overtaken so many of our neighbors. I made a survey of the railroad and recognized how we were allowing the property to suffer in appearance. It occurred to me that simple and good housekeeping offered an offset to some of the shortcuts that we were taking in our maintenance program. The examples I used in talking with my associates were the housekeepers I knew as a boy back in the country, who had so little in the way of tools and equipment, but who kept spotless kitchens. Out of these discussions grew a program to have a place for everything and to keep everything in its place. Shop grounds that had been cluttered began to be models of good housekeeping, and the same was true of stations and yards and even of offices. The good-housekeeping program really caught on and has been continued over the years since then, and it has contributed to safety and economy as well as to appearances.

It may not be so readily apparent why good housekeeping should be an example of putting religion to work. But I believe that whatever contributes to the satisfaction and sense of achievement of the worker on the job is essentially and fundamentally Christian.

Still another example is our suggestion program on the Illinois Central. One of our operating officers, who later became our president, and I supported our suggestion program from the beginning. We had to sell the entire organization on it, because it is the management people up and down the line who want suggestions and have to make them effective for the program to succeed. We were fortunate in winning the support not merely of top management but of the line officers and other supervisors, and our program was a success from the beginning. More than a million dollars has been paid in awards to employees for the suggestions that have been adopted and put into practice, and the experience has been one of the real contributors to the morale of the organization. Some years ago a contest was conducted among railroad employees throughout the country for the best essays on "Why I Like to Work for My Railroad." I was one of the judges of the several hundred essays that were submitted by our employees, and I was struck by the fact that our asking them for suggestions, our giving them a voice in the business of our railroad was mentioned more than any other reason why they liked to work for our railroad. Is this an example of Christian concern and experience in the public relations program of my company? I truly believe it is.

I believe Christian concern has a broad base, a wide field of application. I have been privileged to know a great number of truly dedicated Christian laymen. Many of them are in public relations and are the real leaders of the field. Many of them are men and women whom I have known in business and industry and in the professions. In every instance they have been people who cared for people, who

166

devoted themselves ceaselessly to fostering the kind of relations among their associates that in my opinion is the very essence of good public relations. Such people have been a real inspiration to me throughout my working life. From them I have endeavored to draw inspiration and guidance in facing up to the problems that I have encountered along the way. Everything in my work over the years has been a team effort involving my associates. Truly no man is an island.

MY JOB IS RESEARCH;
MY WORK IS PEOPLE
J. R. Wish

I am a research associate working on a study of economic development sponsored by the Alliance for Progress. But I conceive my work to be much broader than the job description. My job is socio-economic research, but my work is people.

My job, my work, my life are highly interrelated. They are competitive, yet complementary. My job, the source of my salary, lies in some research that I have been doing. My work is what I do with my life. Later I shall discuss some of the specific ties and conflicts between my job and my work.

My Job

Since June, 1965, I have been a member of an interdisciplinary team from Michigan State University. In the first phase of a two-phase research effort we have studied food distribution in Puerto Rico. Some significant changes there in the last fifteen years have resulted in the population and the food supply growing at the same time. This parallel growth is unique in much of Latin America and the world as a whole, where the population is increasing more rapidly than the food supply. Some United States Department of Agriculture production economists have stated that throughout the world the present rate of growth in food supplies is so much lower than the rate of population growth that we will be faced with mass starvation within the next ten to twenty years.

The Food and Agricultural Organization of the United Nations has estimated that just to maintain the present inadequate level, in much of the world, of food supplies, we must double the total agricultural production in the years between 1965 and 1980. Perhaps there is a lesson in the Puerto Rican experience which might be used for increasing the agricultural productivity elsewhere.

Food distribution improvements can mean, indeed are necessary to, an increase in food production. We believe that production will usually increase only as producers learn what foods are needed, as better communication systems are built, and as storage facilities are constructed. All these changes involve distribution.

The rapid change of food distribution methods in Puerto Rico is a part of a rapid economic development. This, too, is tied in with another global issue that faces all of us as human beings. Many of us are interested in erasing some of the inequities that exist in the world. Since food is so important, we believe that understanding food distribution will help us in understanding social change. We are trying especially hard to understand the people who cause the change. How do they differ from the rest?

After the Puerto Rican phase of our study is completed, the results will be disseminated by a conference in a written report. They will be available to anyone who wants them. Some businessmen may see new opportunities as a result of the research. The government of Puerto Rico may use the results of this research in changing the legal environment within which the food distribution firms operate. Also, there is evidence that some other nations could profitably employ parts of the Puerto Rican experience in order to increase agricultural productivity and the nutritional well-being of their people.

In October, 1966, our team expanded for the second phase and moved to two different locations. An interdisciplinary group of agricultural economists, psychologists, marketing specialists, and systems engineers began working closely with local nationals in the poverty-stricken northeastern Brazil area around Recife. I became involved in

Bolivia with another interdisciplinary and multinational team. In both countries we drew upon the research methods which were first tried out in Puerto Rico. In both countries we are working with the United States Agency for International Development, as well as with local persons who are affiliated with local businesses, government offices, and university departments.

Still, exactly what is it that I do and for which I receive my salary? My job carries the title "research associate," which means that I am concerned with particular types of research in association with others. In addition I am the administrative officer for our research project when it is away from the Michigan State University campus. In the next few paragraphs I shall give an approximate breakdown of time on the job, based on 55–70 hours in a 6–6½ day week.

As with many jobs, more could always be done than there is time for. On the average, about twenty percent of my time is devoted to planning research. About half that time is spent alone in tedious, difficult, periods in which I try to sort out meaningful relationships. The other half of the planning is spent in sessions with one to six of my associates. At these meetings we bounce ideas off one another and argue long and hard for particular viewpoints. Out of these sessions and my private periods a new and exciting theory of economic development seems to be taking shape.

Probably fifty percent of my time is concerned with the execution of our plans. This means really three different kinds of work: (1) informal conversations with businessmen, government leaders, or housewives—that is, people who know what is happening in food distribution because they are involved in buying and selling relationships; (2) formal conversations, in the form of questionnaires, with a great number of people involved in food distribution; and (3) searching for already published statistics and other factual descriptions.

About ten percent of my time is spent reading professional journals, books, and pamphlets. The remaining time is devoted to administrative work which involves both people and paper: hiring, counseling, working with my team so we better understand one another; seeing that proper financial reports are filed and overseeing the payment of bills; making sure that the $8,000 revolving account for which I am signed is both available to get the job done and properly managed so that my shirt is not lost. Another important part of the administrative work is helping people fit themselves to the task at hand so that they are doing what they like and like what they are doing.

A small part of the administrative work involves explaining to outsiders why I am convinced people work best when they set their own speed and time. Essentially, I subscribe to McGregor's Theory Y of management. He has dichotomized various views of management under the terms Theory X and Theory Y. A manager who operates under Theory X assumes that people are inherently lazy and need close supervision to make sure they do the job they are paid for. A Theory Y manager, on the other hand, believes that most persons have pride in their work and know best how to accomplish what they are about. The less direct supervision, the better. Still, the Theory Y manager is quite interested in results. He is as willing as, or more willing than, the Theory X manager to weed out incompetence or malingering.

Yet it would be improper and misleading to imply that my job is the be-all and end-all of my life. My life is a free interplay among various claims. For much of those 55–70 hours described above, my horizon is being broadened and I attempt to help others broaden theirs. Thus, my work and my job coincide.

For the remainder of the week, sometimes less and sometimes more, there are responsibilities to my family, friends, and relatives as well as myself. It is frequently difficult to attempt to make rational decisions concerning allocations of time. Often the demands of the job and those of loved ones conflict. It is important to follow through on one's commitment to his child. Part of my work is being a good father. Yet my job is a large part of my life and therefore of my work. Frequently it is difficult to know which of the tasks facing me is the most important. The most urgent may not be the most important. The writing of this paper has meant spending less time with my wife and children. My seven-year-old daughter is certain that there were things like bicycle rides and story reading that were both more urgent and more important. Perhaps she is right. But there are emotional, moral, and spiritual ties beyond myself which help me believe I made the proper choice.

My Beliefs

Christian Existentialism: Reality requires that I make some decisions and that I consciously or subconsciously state and think about relations with my fellowman and with my God. Some friends have said that I am an existentialist. I do agree with Sartre who said that "every truth and every action implies a human setting and a human subjectivity." However, I consider myself more than an existentialist who follows Sartre. With Sartre, I agree that "man is responsible for what he is" and that he is responsible not only for himself as an individual but "that he is responsible for all men."

But, more than this, as a Christian existentialist I believe that, even though man is responsible for what he is (i.e., he really does have free will), he has, beyond that, a responsibility to his fellowman based upon a responsibility to God through Jesus Christ. This basis in God does not in any way abrogate my other responsibilities; rather, it makes my responsibilities to myself and to my fellowman that much more meaningful. This responsibility to God means that there is another factor pulling on me, a questioning of what is God's will and how is God using me in this situation. Furthermore, a Christian existentialist does, I believe, form at least a part of his life as a response to God's plan through Jesus Christ.

Some people object to the term "Christian existentialist" and claim that one can be either a Christian or an existentialist but not both. To me, that argument would be valid only if we had received complete revelation from God, of his plan and his will both for each individual life and for the world as a whole.

The great diversity of Christian sects is an indication that God has *not* revealed all of himself to any one man. In the field of civil rights, the variety of stands taken *with honest conviction* suggests that being a Christian is not following a set of rules to the extent some would have us believe. And finally, at the time of this writing when the Viet Nam conflict looms large, there is no unity of prescriptions of what a concerned Christian and a citizen of the United States ought to do.

I don't know the correct course in any of these situations. Yet decisions must be made. In each of the examples the responsible person is bound to do *something*. Thus, if one is a Christian and makes choices, even if he is not certain beyond a shadow of a doubt of the "rightness" of his choices, he could consider himself a "Christian existentialist" who believes that there is a God who has a plan and that events occur for a reason.

Types of Decisions: There are two kinds of decisions with which I am faced, *routine decisions* and *non-routine decisions*.

Routine decisions I define as mechanical decisions, such as stopping for a red light or ordering more paper for the office. These are the decisions that can be subjected to a computer technology, they are the yes-no type decisions. Because these decisions are mechanical, technology and machines can help me decide. The weight of making these is to some extent removed, just as the repetitive assembly-line factory work is being removed for better handling by automated machines.

The things that really matter are the non-routine decisions. And at some time or another we are all faced with these. It was a non-routine decision that Abraham made when he heard the voice of God commanding him to sacrifice his son on the mountaintop. Abraham, as you remember, had to make a decision. He was faced with the horrible dilemma that if it was the voice of God and he did not obey it, he had committed blasphemy. On the other hand, if it was not the voice of God but he did obey it, he had perpetrated a most awful murder. He had to make a decision not knowing the outcome, not really knowing God's will. Each of us frequently finds himself in the position of Abraham.

Assumptions and Guidelines

What is it that guides one to face the alternatives and fearlessly make non-routine decisions?

As a scientist I subscribe to the view that we really "know" only those relationships that have been proved false and those that have not yet been proved false. Truth we do not "know." As one of my friends sometimes jokingly remarks, "The good Lord has not seen fit to reveal all the truth to any one man." If we do not "know truth," we must accept as valid some or all of the things "not yet proved false" in order to function. Such an outlook should keep a person humble and open to new interpretations. But such an outlook could immobilize one and prevent him from taking action, prevent him from making decisions if he did not have faith and a belief that decisions must be made.

Secondly, we impose structure upon reality. We see things in certain patterns. Social science research has indicated that human beings search for patterns in relationships and find meaning even when there definitely are not any as determined by "objective standards." Thus we have different ways of looking at events and looking at reality.

Also, there may be more than one correct way of looking at things. The early scientific view was that if man, in looking for the way God put the world together, could just get enough time or adequate measuring devices he would be able to understand all that was possible and thus would become God-like. My own view today is that, while there may or may not be an actual structure and meaning to the universe, I assume one in order to better understand what is going on. Again, this gives me a sense of humility and appreciation for my fellowman's viewpoint, because neither of our views has yet been proved false.

Furthermore, I believe that a certain amount of competition or conflict is a good thing. Competition and conflict seem to bring out both the best and the worst in us human beings. (I am bothered by the fact that too much competition or too much conflict seems as bad as, if not worse than, too little.) However, I am convinced that in many cases too little competition or conflict means stagnation, and to me stagnation means lack of change which implies death.

Then, too, some minimum level of material possessions

is necessary for a person to live like a human being. There seems to be some substance to the argument that the more material possessions a man has, the more he is able to consider various alternatives for living a better life, for serving his fellowman, or being degenerate if he so chooses. For example, a starving man has few alternatives that mean anything to him. It certainly is foolish to talk to him about political freedom, or to talk to him about Jesus Christ.

Another guideline underlying my view of reality is that, within the limitations imposed by time and money, it is always good to attempt to find out more about the people and things in our lives, to try to advance knowledge, to subject everything to question. I believe that God is at work in the world, leading toward some plan which I don't know. There is a considerable amount of evidence on the side of the meaninglessness of existence and the impossibility of change for the better if man doesn't use his free will to do things. There is evidence that man makes many errors and that what seems to be an advance sometimes is not. I am as unwilling to accept the fatalistic view of the conservative Christian as that of the atheistic humanist.

Some Major Decisions That I Face

The toughest decision that faces me as a responsible human being is my allocation of time. As an individual who is happily married and has three lovely children, lives in a community, and has a job—what are my *responsibilities* to myself and to those about me? How much time do I

178

spend with my family? How much time should I spend on the job for which I am paid? How much time should I spend in my church? How much time should I spend in community activities? No religion, no other person can make this decision for me, neither can I attempt to make this decision for others.

Another decision that I must make comes when I find myself (or think I find myself) being "used" by another person. What is my reaction to be? Is it to be a Christian reaction of turning the other cheek, or should I retaliate? It seems that retaliation has its place. Yet there is certainly a tension between retaliation and non-violence. "There is only one thing worse than being killed, and that's being alive when you should be dead," says one of my friends. And one's death can come from non-violence as well as from retaliation.

A further issue which bothers me is how to maintain a Christian concern and love for other individuals without becoming physically and emotionally too involved. Perhaps this question can be asked another way. How far should I become emotionally or physically involved with those outside my biological family? What are the social, economic, and psychological consequences to me and to others?

Some people say that Christians should be disinterested with no thoughts of acquiring selfish ends. But how can you express Christian concern without being involved? It is only when you become involved *as means to a selfish end* that your involvement is not Christian. But I frequently don't know what is selfish, and I can't express concern without involvement.

Another problem is: What am I as an individual to do when I disagree with the way my country is going? (One might substitute "corporation," "university," "labor union," or any other organization of which he is a part.) For instance, if I disagree with my nation's involvement in Viet Nam, what should I as a citizen do about it?

These are some of the major decisions that my life requires me to reflect upon. They are decisions that I think many people are required to face as responsible human beings. It is much easier not to think about them. To the extent that computers and various other technological devices come into the fore to take over routine decision making and routine jobs, we human beings will have more time to think about these major decisions.

Christian Dimensions

Christian dimensions are interwoven in all these questions and should be interwoven throughout my entire life. They are contained in three words. These words express "oughts," and not how I actually live from day to day. They express how I would hope to live. These words are *love, humility,* and *justice.*

Love, humility, and justice facilitate the process of becoming. Love, humility, and justice help one lose himself in something more meaningful than the self. I have sometimes been accused of being cocksure and at the same time wanting to wear the cloak of humility.

I am not, and probably never will be, the person I would like to be. Still, for me, it is necessary to strive toward the things that seem important: to do a good job in my teaching and in my research; to be a loving, concerned, compassionate husband to my wife; to be a good example and teacher to my children so that they can increasingly make choices for themselves; to be responsible to my biological family; to be available to others who want to discuss or do something else about their life span; to make some contribution to my nation.

To accomplish any of these objectives requires actions and non-routine decisions. I realize that some of my actions may be the result of my selfishness. I realize that actions may be wrong. Frequently I won't know about it until after damage has been done.

For me, a meaningful, viable life is one that is always in the process of becoming. This implies never being mature, if being mature means being unwilling to change or having "the answers." A viable and meaningful life also implies a certain amount of conflict. Some suggest to relax and not deal with incipient conflicts. But avoidance of conflict can be the coward's way out.

There seem to be many paradoxes and dilemmas in life. Life is uncertain. We are told God is at work in the world, but if he is, why is there so much hate, injustice, and pain? On the other hand, some would have us believe that life is absurd and without meaning; but, if it is, why the moments of true love, selfless service, and miracles?

For me as for others, the freedom to make decisions is at times a horrendous burden. Camus expresses it clearly in *The Fall*:

Freedom is not a reward or a decoration that is celebrated with champagne. Nor yet a gift, a box of dainties designed to make you lick your chops. Oh no! It's a chore . . . and a long-distance race, quite solitary and very exhausting. . . . At the end of all freedom is a court sentence; that's why freedom is too heavy to bear, especially when you're down with a fever, or are distressed, or love nobody.

But if there are no ground rules for decisions, and if with freedom I may err, I much prefer that the mistakes be my own rather than those of others.

Throughout, I have spoken with more assurance than may be justified. I am gravely uncertain at times.

LAY THEOLOGY
—A SYNOPSIS   *Frederick K. Wentz*

The preceding chapters are presented as inherently interesting to the reader. They were called forth and have been
published as ideas and experiences that would be suggestively
helpful to other laymen who want to be Christian in their
daily work. No further justification for this volume is needed.

Is There Such a Thing?

Nonetheless, in retrospect, these chapters illustrate a little-
recognized but significant fact: that *there is a major phenom-*
enon in the Christian life which can be called lay theology.

The term "lay theology" does not mean a theology about laymen, nor does it refer to the watering down of formal, technical theology so that laymen can comprehend it. If theology be defined as the coherent interpretation of Christian data, then lay theology can be defined as *the coherent interpretation of their life-style which laymen develop from their own experiences in gospel-world encounter.* By this definition it would be clear that there is no one lay theology; rather, there are many lay theologies.

It is my claim that professional theologians have, for the most part, either ignored such lay theologies or summarily dismissed them as amateurish, biased, or otherwise inadequate,[1] whereas they should be a central element in all theological efforts for our day.

One reason for this failure is that lay theology is quite hard for the professional theologian to find. When the preceding chapters reached my desk, one by one, I scrutinized them as a seminary professor and concluded that, with a couple of notable exceptions, there was little theology in them, and what was there was shallow. However, on second reading I modified my judgment in two ways. I found many more of the explicit phrases of formal theology than I remembered from the first inspection. But more significantly, recalling that I had specifically asked these people to start with daily work and *then* bring in their faith, I realized that these statements represented for each person a working philosophy of life, a rationale for his various commitments,

[1] With such notable exceptions as T. S. Eliot and Dag Hammarskjöld.

a description of a style of life, a genuinely functional theology. It is with such material that the professional theologian should start his work. But it is very hard for him to see it, even when it has been dug out for him—partly because it seems to have so little to do with the patterns of formal theology.

I hope that someday somebody with a hidden tape recorder will go around and talk to professional theologians about how they operate, how they schedule writing time at their desks, how they accept lecture appointments, how they shape their careers and handle their students. It would be interesting to see in what manner the phrases of formal theology enter into *that* story!

What Are They Saying?

As a group the writers of the foregoing chapters can be described as committed Christians. They also obviously have a strong commitment to their occupations. In fact most of them were brought to the editor's attention because they combined these two characteristics with the ability to articulate their thoughts and experiences. As a group they are also, like their editor, American, Protestant, non-fundamentalist.

Beyond that, they are almost a random selection. An effort has been made to secure a variety of occupations and some geographical spread. But little effort has been given to securing any overall balance, for example, in sex, age, education, or class level.

A notable fact about these chapters is the variety of their viewpoints. No two of them take the same approach. The two public relations men, for example, contrast quite sharply in their treatments. The one, a retired railroad executive, looks back over his career and finds little of conflict or ambiguity of decision—his specific tasks appear to him to have fed directly into the common good. The other, getting his own business underway, believes in his role but sees many dilemmas and many tortured decisions in combining occupational success with Christian convictions. Such variety, I believe, is inherent in lay theology, especially as worked out by American Protestant individualists. In my judgment the rich diversity is one of the virtues of this volume.

Yet, clearly, there are significant common themes running through the chapters. One of the explicit theological themes is that of creation, stressing that this whole world is God's, and that he is active in the business world or wherever one works. Another is stewardship, emphasizing that one must use his God-given talents to participate in creation by developing those skills, materials, and opportunities that one has. A third is vocation, tying together God's call to be a Christian and one's occupation as a worthwhile task in the name of human betterment. The ideals of meeting human needs, providing personal care for other people, seeking fulfillment for all men, or aiding in the growth of human beings are strong motifs in these essays.

Large sections of this volume have been written under the assumption that ethical decisions are the primary way in which one's faith-commitment is related to his weekday tasks. For the most part these chapters are not taken up with a narrow code morality; more often the appeal is to the complexities of the situation, to the need for responsible human relationships, and to the requirements of such general values as love, truth, integrity, individual freedom, justice, and humility. Consensus in controversy, sensitivity toward other groups, forgiveness—these values are mentioned but appear less often. Considerable emphasis is put upon the dignity of man, the worth of the individual, the importance of individual initiative, the right of personal self-determination. Several of the writers include the defeat of communism as an important goal. All in all they reflect a distinctly American ethos and value system.

This raises the question of ideology. Do the authors simply line up ideas and values to be used as weapons for defending their own biases and prior investments? Nobody's announced philosophy or theology avoids some ideological warping; one can suspect that this element is reflected in some of the assertions on these pages. But there is evidence in every essay that the ideas affirmed have also shaped the writer's decisions and style of life to some extent. In my judgment the preceding chapters rate rather high for honesty in this respect.

More explicit than the ideological note is the way in which this volume illustrates the traditional "Protestant ethic," i.e., the belief in the value of individual initiative and hard work, together with the tendency to find God's blessing associated with occupational excellence. These Protestants do take their jobs seriously and, with one exception, do relate this attitude to their Christian faith. They have a high sense of professional responsibility; they want to uphold the code of their profession and enhance the role their group plays. Or they stress the importance of their trade for the progress of civilization or the proper supplying of human needs.

Sometimes the emphasis is upon the job itself, in which the author finds meanings that others seldom find. More often the occupation is a means to some other end. Broad service to humanity is often the end toward which daily tasks are thought to be directed. Frequently the writer stresses his opportunities to help his fellow workers or other individuals or groups immediately involved in the daily routine. Most of the essays, on the other hand, appear to be deficient in an emphasis on significant change in the social structure—seldom is the job viewed as a way to alter the social fabric itself.

The Church and Lay Theology

Several of the writers make explicit what is implicit throughout: the organized church does not provide much specific support for lay Christians at their jobs. The realtor likens his experience to the man who plants a flag on a mountain peak in a howling snowstorm and finds himself "with no supply trains, little or no communication, and slim chance ever to return to the home base."

It should surprise nobody, therefore, to discover that from the standpoint of formal theology the preceding pages, on the average, are slim pickings. This volume is simply another evidence that the gap between books on theology and the working place of laymen is deep and wide. This fact does not put in question the validity of the Christian thought and action described in this book; it only indicates a failure in providing full resources for these Christian tasks.

In a larger sense, of course, the preceding chapters reflect Christian thinking. If they could be compared with similar expressions, for example of Asian Buddhists, these chapters would give evidence of the Judeo-Christian tradition (as well as the traditions of Western civilization and America). This makes all the more tragic the split between these essays and the writings of formal theology. Each needs the other. With more formal theology these laymen could purge and deepen their experiences of the Christian life. With more attention to such lay theology the church and her theologians would be much more effective in relating the gospel to the realities of modern life.

In fact, a call for such a shift in the focus of the church's intellectual endeavor is part of Bishop J. A. T. Robinson's challenge in *The New Reformation?* [2] Using the thinking of Charles Davis, he refers to four major theological "cultures" in church history. One is episcopal theology, written mainly by bishops and expressing the church's pastoral concern. A second is monastic and grows out of contemplation and the mystical life. A third is scholastic and grows out of the university setting. A fourth is "seminary theology" which has been shaped for the training of a professional clergy. Bishop

[2] (Philadelphia: The Westminster Press, 1965), chap. 3.

Robinson suggests that our age demands a fifth type, namely, lay theology. By this he does not mean the theologizing done by laymen (as we have met it in this book) but the professional theologizing that emerges out of the needs and experiences of laymen. As he puts it, "a theology which is impelled by the needs of the *laos*, or whole people of God, to *be* the Church *in* the world." Its creative source would be "the engagement of the *laos* in the life of the world." [3] Such a lay theology would be more comprehensive and rigorous than the dozen chapters of this book. But these chapters would provide some of the basic materials to which such a formal lay theology would address itself.

There is an urgent need for a lay theology (in Bishop Robinson's use of that term). At the same time there is much valuable lay theological material and there are many lay theologies (in our use of that phrase to mean the coherent interpretation of their experiences by laymen). A dozen of them are set forth in this volume. They—together with many others that could be called forth—are the raw materials which the modern church should ponder with penetration, if she is to understand her existence as the agent of God's mission and is to shape her message wisely for today's world.

[3] *Ibid.*, p. 63.

CONTRIBUTORS

Cecelia Newbold (Mrs. Vernon W.)
  Registered Nurse
  Denver, Colorado
  United Church of Christ

Norman E. Madson
  Partner in Architectural Firm of Sövik, Mathre & Madson
  Northfield, Minnesota
  Lutheran

Louis R. Mobley
  Manager of Education and Development, Federal Systems Division,
    IBM Corporation
  Ellicott City, Maryland
  Methodist

Carroll Thompson
  President, Carroll Thompson Co., Inc. (Public Relations)
  Lincoln, Nebraska
  Lutheran

Dallas Sells
  President, Indiana State AFL-CIO
  Indianapolis, Indiana
  Baptist

Elliott Couden
President, Couden Agency, Inc. (Realtors)
Seattle, Washington
United Church of Christ

Jan J. Erteszek
President, Olga Company
Van Nuys, California
Congregationalist

Richard C. Waybright
Part Owner and One of Managers of Mason Dixon Farms, Inc.
Gettysburg, Pennsylvania
Lutheran

Paul Wilbor
Retired Civilian Employee of the Department of Defense of the
U. S. Government
Arlington, Virginia
Episcopalian

Nadine A. Oyler
Household Helper
Gettysburg, Pennsylvania
Lutheran

George M. Crowson
Retired Assistant to the President of Illinois Central Railroad
Chicago, Illinois
United Church of Christ

John R. Wish
Assistant Professor, Latin American Market Planning Center
(Bolivia) of Michigan State University
Washington, D. C.
Presbyterian

Frederick K. Wentz
President, Hamma School of Theology
Springfield, Ohio
Lutheran

My Job
and My Faith

●

FREDERICK K. WENTZ, Editor

These twelve candid self-portraits of ordinary men and women and their jobs will help all of us see a more vital relationship between faith and work. They will enable ministers and theologians to understand more accurately the needs and motivations of the persons to whom they minister.

Each report is personal—guided only by several questions asked by the editor. Each reflects the innermost thoughts on faith and the demands of the working day.

Common themes recur: Man's responsibility in the ongoing creativity of God; man's stewardship of his talents in this creation; and the idea of vocation, tying together faith and work. The meeting of human need, providing care for others, and seeking a full life for all people are other strong motifs.

The author adds a final chapter in which he envisions the need for a truly "lay" theology, one based on interpreting the life-style which laymen develop from their experiences in gospel-life encounter.

ABINGDON PRESS